# LIVING IN CONCORD

### Essays, Reflections, Memoirs, a Poem and a Recipe

## Jim Leahy

Living in Concord; Essays, Reflections, Memoirs, a
Poem and a Recipe

Copyright © 2007 by Jim Leahy

Debra's Natural Gourmet, Publisher
98 Commonwealth Avenue,
Concord, MA 01742
978-371-7573

ISBN 978-0-9742627-1-0

This book is offered with thanks to many people for their support over the years. Special thanks to David Stark for his invaluable assistance and guidance with the layout and design; to Lewis Rice, Greg Turner, Maureen O'Connell and Cheryl Lecesse, successive editors over the last ten years at *The Concord Journal,* and Betsy Levinson, the editor at *The Littleton Independent,* who have been willing to publish my columns; to Debra Stark and all my friends at Debra's Natural Gourmet for believing in me; to my father and mother and my two brothers for providing the loving background from which I grew; and most especially to my dear wife Diane for a lifetime of support and encouragement and love.

# Contents

INTRODUCTION                              9

TO MY FATHER                             13

TIPS TO BEAT THE WINTER                  15

IN THE GAP                               19

DULCE DOMUM IN CONCORD                   23

REMEMBERING MY FATHER                    27

INDEPENDENCE DAY                         31

PERENNIAL MYSTERIES                      35

ORGANIC MONTH IN CONCORD                 39

THANKS FOR THE MEMORIES                  43

TRAVELLERS ALL                           47

BENEATH THE DREAMING SPIRES              51

A CHILD'S CHRISTMAS IN ENGLAND           57

DANDELION DAYS                           61

DEPARTURES                               65

THE LAST MOWS OF SUMMER                  69

IN THE DEEP MIDWINTER                    73

SURE A LITTLE BIT OF HEAVEN              77

ARE WE THERE YET?                        81

DANCING WITH THE DAFFODILS   85

CYCLES OF LIFE   89

VACATION MEMORIES   93

PLAIN SAILING   97

THE PRIZE   103

LETTING GO   107

FOR AULD LANG SYNE   113

EQUINOX   117

TEACHERS   121

THOSE DYING GENERATIONS   125

AFTER THANKSGIVING   129

HYACINTHS & HOLLYHOCKS   133

AGING PICTURES   137

A FATHER'S DAY MEMORY   141

SEASONAL CYCLES   147

LIVING IN CONCORD   151

# INTRODUCTION

The idea for this book first came to me in November of 2004. Encouraged by friend and fellow *Concord Journal* columnist, Glenn Rifkin, who had just published his own anthology of musings, *Thoreau's Backyard*, I began to consider doing the same. I had begun writing occasionally for the newspaper in 1997, contributing columns about small business, in which I have a vital interest, and about the people of our town in a series titled Faces of Concord. I spent many pleasant hours talking to some of my fellow citizens, and I learned much about living in Concord from them.

At the turn of the millennium, I began to write these more personal reflections. It was not until four years into this process that I ever considered anthologizing them. There was never any intended unity to my writing until then, and while I have held the intention of this book since that time, even the subsequent columns were written as stand-alone pieces. Any unity to this work is more discovered than designed. Because they emanate from one writer's mind, a mind which tends to circulate around the same themes and not infrequently expresses itself with repetition, there are themes which I as a reader of my own work have found in them.

Because each piece was written as a column to stand in its own right, and because there is a certain chronology which occasionally emerges through them, as I refer from time to time to the passage of the years, I have decided, with one exception, to arrange the columns chronologically as written, in order not to confuse any reader with erratic backward and forward shifts in the narrative time. I also decided to show the date on which each column was written in order to maintain that clarity.

Any other attempt to organize the book seemed to me like a vain attempt to force a structure onto this project, rather than to simply allow these writings to coalesce into their own form.

Perhaps my one attempt to summarize the book as some kind of a unified expression came in choosing a title, and in writing an individual column which bears that title. For this reason I placed that column as the final chapter. As I looked over my work of the last seven years it seemed to me that what most seemed to engage me was the experience of trying to live in the present with the past. I have always been keenly aware of the transience of life, and have experienced the passage through my years with feelings of loss. As an immigrant, my heritage, my family, my memories have been of great import to me, even as I live in the present, experiencing and embracing the moments of my life.

Thus, living in Concord for me has meant living in concord: between past and present, between my native and my adopted ways. It has also meant living in concord with my beliefs, with my community, with nature, finding the harmony of who I am and who I have become.

Writing for *The Concord Journal* has been a rewarding experience. When I began, I had only ever written for myself or for family or for friends. The lure of publication was enticing. The concept of a little fame even in a small town was enticing. Along the way, I have discovered that it has been most satisfying to be read by those who know me, and because I spend my days in the public place of a natural food store, Debra's Natural Gourmet, I have had the privilege of being received and appreciated by more than a few people. I have found that to be read by people I know is infinitely more rewarding than to be read by strangers. For this I am very grateful. The encouragement I have been given has in large part given me the inspiration to produce this book, so I offer it to all those who have shown their support along the way, and helped me to believe that the musings of my meandering and circling mind are still worth expressing.

# TO MY FATHER

You are the leaf that's fallen from the tree,
Your body surrendered to the ground,
The life that passed through you
New forming
On the tree.

You are the song now still,
Sound faded out of time,
A song I'll hear no more,
But which I sing each day.

You are my brother's smile,
My arms around my wife.
Once contained and easy to find
You were.
Now I seek you everywhere.

# TIPS TO BEAT THE WINTER
## February 2000

Shortly after Valentine's Day each year my wife, Diane, and I walk over to the linden tree at the corner of our yard to look for the first sign of spring: crocus tips. Once again we found them there this year. Just enough to have pushed aside the soil, the first few have appeared, their hopeful heads not yet above the ground, but visible in the crack. Unlike the groundhog, they will not see their shadow and retreat, but will remain and grow, imperceptibly at first, hidden under the recent snow that has returned to cover them. When their six weeks of winter have passed they will bring us our first blooms of whites and yellows and striated purples. And then they will be gone. Three years ago they waved in seventy-degree Easter Sunday breezes before succumbing to two feet of spring snow on Monday, April Fool's Day. The following year I watched them wilt in ninety-degree March heat. Perhaps this year they will be washed away by the spring rains, or maybe they will run their course through gentler sun and showers, but they will give way to daffodils and tulips, scilla and peony, lady's mantle, nepeta, evening primrose, daylilies.

In July when we look out of our kitchen window, we will see each day for a few weeks the same daylilies, 'Dance Ballerina

Dance', 'Phaedra', 'Gold Thimble', 'Rachel's Hope'. Yet every blossom will be new each day, to live for one day, as yesterday's falls from the stem and tomorrow's waits in the bud. My inexpert eye will be fooled, as always, into thinking I am seeing the same plant, when I will, in fact, be looking at something for the first time each day.

So it is as I approach seven times seven years on this earth; every particle of my body will have been replaced seven times. What remains of the original me conceived in the Autumn of 1951, brought into the light of day in June of 1952, while my father, banished to picking peas in our Oxford back garden, anxiously awaited the first cries from the bedroom upstairs, where my mother lay attended by my grandmother and Nurse Godfrey the midwife? A pattern of energy, a code by which these ever-changing cells have brought me to the present?

My first memory, my brother Nigel's birth in 1955, still lives in me. "Can it talk?" I asked, and still I feel myself standing before the crib in the corner, watching the sleeping baby, as if the grown-up me was compressed whole into a three-year-old's body, like a flower inside a bulb.

Season passes upon season, waves lap onto the shore, college years follow school years, a career unfolds, loved ones die, the pear tree that Diane and I planted when we bought our house now towers twenty feet high in our border, gray hairs begin to grow more thickly, children are born. Sometimes when standing beside the ocean, I sense that I can feel, not see or understand, but feel the pattern, the wholeness. It has never had meaning for me. There is too much random cruelty and sorrow for me to find benevolence in it, but in some way I am comforted by my own insignificance, as well as by some strange sense of belonging. To be a part of it all is enough. To share it is more than enough. All pain, all worry will eventually be washed to nothingness. Like the discarded particles of my body, they will be absorbed into the stars. Only the present moment will remain. To hold hands and to gaze into the infinite night sky, love can fill the moment; all else is erased by the vast and mysterious oneness.

Nevertheless, I miss my father. Eighteen years ago (that seem like yesterday) he died. In eighteen years, which will seem shorter than the last eighteen no doubt, I will have reached the age at which he died. In so many ways he still lives in me, in memory, thought and action, and when he died, too young at 66, I knew his life was whole and just as precious as if it were a longer life, but I would like to take him out to see the crocuses bloom, even though the only flowers he could name were the daisies which he battled in his lawn. I would like to stand beside him watching the tide come in and out again along the Dorset coast, where he last lived.

It is impossible not to grieve for all the lost moments of our lives, the friends we have known, the family members who have passed on, the wedding-day long past, the knowledge that we all one day will be separated from our mortal coil, whatever we may understand that to mean. All things will pass. All our moments we will hold as memories. All joy will also entail sorrow.

I only rarely succeed in taking my own advice. It is too hard to live in the present moment fully, never to fear the coming changes, never to anticipate the partings. I look back. I look forward. Watching the crocus tips breaking through the ground, I see another winter falling away behind me. From spring we shall move to summer. The red-gold leaves of fall will soon enough be sweeping through the fading garden. As each season passes I shall try to embrace as many moments as I can: running my hand through the first warm and turgid grasses of the spring, putting my nose to the peony before the June rain that so often comes to turn it to mush the day after it opens, appreciating each morning's unique new crop of daylilies, inhaling the scents of fall's decay. All the while the clouds will move across the sky, the sun will rise and set, and next year I will take my self out, new cells and old, to look for the tell-tale tip.

# IN THE GAP
## March 2000

I had had one eye on the odometer for a while, so I was aware that we were approaching 100,000 miles. It was on a Wednesday morning, February 24, when my wife, Diane, was leaving for Lexington, that I considered the distance and reminded her to notice on the way home. She made it back with two miles still to go. So as I headed down to Thoreau Street (one mile away) later that afternoon, I knew that I would observe the changeover on the way back home.

As I approached the driveway of our house, slowly, because my gaze kept deflecting to the odometer, I saw all the nines beginning to shift upwards. Creeping onto the asphalt and stopping the car on its spot before the garage door, I stared with some wonder at the numbers displayed before me. Caught in the moment of transition, the car came to rest with the tails of all the nines ascending out of view as the tops of all the zeroes rose up from below.

For those of us eccentric enough to pay attention to these little moments in life, it might seem quite remarkable. How many people reach that milestone parked in the driveway of their own home? How often do we capture any moment in our lives, pausing exactly in the gap between past and future? Since we had purchased the car on Valentine's Day of 1990, it marked ten years and ten days of ownership, the length of ten medieval courtly quests. What kinds of meanings could I layer onto all this?

Time for an oil change? That seemed a little mundane. I'm rather too much of a believer in randomness to ascribe great significance to the coincidences that life so often throws our way, but I do like to use them for a little reflection. For here I am in the middle of my life, after 25 years in the same job, on the verge of a major career shift, as it happens, and very aware of being in that uncomfortable in-between space myself. At the end of one long journey and the beginning of another.

As I embark on my own quest now, I see both the fullness of the receding nines of my life to this point, and a future which can look as frighteningly blank sometimes as a series of zeroes. Much as I like to believe that I should embrace the moments of life, not all the moments are as cuddly as others.

What is the moment anyway, but a nothingness, the conjunction of what has passed and what is yet to be? Is it the conjunction of contentment and hope, or of loss and fear? For the luckiest of us I suspect it is both, and a somewhat tangled conjunction at that.

I am one of those who does not particularly value change. Find me a nice place to vacation and I will go there for ten years. Diane and I hope to see out our lifetimes in our house.

I have a great appetite for familiarity and constancy, and while change is growth, I know, so is steadfastness. Those who run away do not grow faster than those who stay.

Now caught in this gap between past and present, I am reminded that, even though we do not perceive it at all times, this is the nature of life, always to be on the balance point of unknowing. We, ourselves, who are more space than substance, as science now teaches us, more nothing than something, nourished by memories and dreams, exist, it seems, in the ephemeral conjunction of two non-existent states. No wonder we want to smell the roses.

Of course, I would like to preserve the roses also. "And why not?" I ask myself. For while I exhort myself to live fully in the present, I do not feel that I must abandon hope (or memory) to enter here. History teaches us so often, that there are things which must not be forgotten. There are many torches to be carried to ensure our future. In these gaps we see our past before it slips away, just as we see and feel the beginnings of what is to come.

If we are to live responsibly we need our master planning committees, our goals and our dreams, just as we need our lessons learned.

So as I watch the tails of nines and tops of zeroes and the space between them, as I see one part of my life passing, and the new waiting to unfold, I shall attempt, with many slips no doubt, life's great challenge: to remember the past, to be mindful of the future and to live in the present.

And meanwhile, I had better change that oil.

# DULCE DOMUM IN CONCORD
## May 2000

I have long identified with the Mole in Kenneth Grahame's *The Wind in the Willows*. I first realized this some years ago when, not long in this country, I had recently revisited my home in England. Like the Mole I had hurriedly forsaken and not sought it again, and like the Mole, when recapturing its scent, I had felt "the mysterious fairy call" and the full flood of recollection, the "plaintive reminder that it was there."

Twenty-some years later, as I chance to read the book again, I find once more the Mole speaks for me. For the last several months, I have been preparing for the day that now has arrived, in which my twenty-five years at Concord Spice & Grain are to come to an end, as the store prepares to close its doors for the last time.

Finding a new career after so long in one position is not a comfortable task. It is fraught with many questions. How great a change should one make? What are the most important values to be carried forward? Should I somehow, at almost fifty, try to begin the teaching career for which I thought I was preparing when I went to college in 1970, and with which I have intermittently dabbled through Community Education for some seventeen years?  Can I turn my one idea per month, which *The Concord Journal* is willing to publish, into fame and fortune through national syndication?

Well, once all the fantasies have subsided, the tentative explorations into unknown realms, I come back to myself.  The world may be my oyster, but I am a vegetarian!

"So, who am I?" I ask.  What has been more important to me over the years than to live and work in my own community?  What is more significant in one's work than to express one's values, do something one believes in?

Living amongst Concord's literary and intellectual luminaries, many of whom I greet each day in my role of shopkeeper, it is tempting to aspire to some more prominent or illustrious position in the world.  In truth, however, I could not wish to be a better man than my father, whose greatness resided in love and kindness, in going to work each day and raising a family.

So, I shall go to work each day in my new position at Debra's Natural Gourmet.  I shall continue to work within the town of Concord, to spend my days a mere two miles from home, to continue to promote health and nutrition awareness, support organic growing practices and help provide for the basic needs of the citizens of our town, to work in a way consistent with my own philosophy of environmental and social responsibility. In integrating the basic values long held by both stores, I also attempt to integrate the parts of my life into one meaningful whole.

Like my friend the Mole, who after a period of time away from home finally went to visit the home of Mr. Badger, and found that it exactly suited him, because they were creatures of like domains, so, too, shall I hope to find all that I need in the familiar. Like Henry David Thoreau travelling widely in Concord, I can still "direct [my] eyesight inward, and...find a thousand regions in [my] mind."

I cannot deny that I am drawn to the familiar with its illusions of safety and security. There is excitement enough for me in the daily business of living. The same wind that blew through the willows across the street from us, throwing limbs and branches at our house, was also fanning the flames of a one hundred acre brush fire but a quarter of a mile away in Walden Woods.

If I wish to live as well as my father, then I shall find challenge enough to know myself, to seek to live with kindness, generosity and humility, to accept who I am, to live my values rather than aspire to those of others.

When the Mole leaves the Badger's home and anticipates eagerly a return to his own known world, to the things he knows and likes, he perceives clearly that he is "an animal of tilled field and hedgerow, linked to the ploughed furrow, the frequented pasture, the lane of evening lingerings, the cultivated garden-plot."

Knowing himself thus, his thoughts continue, expressed in Grahame's tender prose. "For others the asperities, the stubborn endurance, or the clash of actual conflict, that went with nature in the rough; he must be wise, must keep to the pleasant places in which his lines were laid and which held adventure enough, in their way, to last for a lifetime."

# REMEMBERING MY FATHER
## June 2000

My father's birthday falls most years just halfway between two moveable feasts, Memorial Day and Father's Day. Born in 1916 in Cork City in the middle of the First World War, his first memories were of Ireland's "troubles". As a young child evacuated briefly to his aunt's house outside the city center, he watched the raging fires set by the departing paramilitary Black and Tans, who proudly strutted through the town wearing pieces of burnt cork behind their ears, a cruel symbol of their parting gift to the new free state.

He crossed over to England during the Second World War to help the war effort in the factories of Oxford. A comedian, a song-and-dance man, he met my mother, a ballerina, entertaining American troops stationed outside the town. They married shortly after the war was over. When he died of heart failure in 1982 on Veteran's Day, peace was still a distant hope, a shattered hope, for his emerald isle.

I will never forget the smell of his hospital room that November morning. I don't know if it was the fluid draining from his lungs into the bottle beside the bed, or if it was something else in the room, the smell of death itself, perhaps, but I can taste it still. Disembarking hurriedly from the plane from

Boston, driven to Bournemouth in the south of England by my brother, Nigel, I arrived to share the last few moments of his consciousness.

He was unable to utter any sounds, but the movement of his lips, the fondness in his eyes told me all I could have wanted to hear, and in the few moments that we had I could speak to him through my shock and tears. Twenty-four hours later, after a morphine-induced sleep, he passed away, and as we all reached for him, my mother, my two brothers and I, he awoke, it seemed, for one last gasp and passed again.

Eighteen years later the loss is softened by the fondness of the memories of his life, and I count myself among the fortunate. Fortunate that love existed in our family life, fortunate that it lay close enough to the surface to be felt and expressed even if with the reserve that characterized our clan, and fortunate that I had somehow chosen to give voice to it just a month before, when I had visited England to attend the wedding of my brother, Sean, and his wife, Viv.

It was the last evening of my stay, and as I sat with my parents, did some foreknowledge prompt me to speak? Younger as I was then, I craved to break through the barrier of our unspoken love, and, perhaps, to assuage my guilt at having left the family to emigrate to a home 3,000 miles across the ocean. And so I told my parents that I loved them. It was a small speech, not very eloquent, reserved, even embarrassed.

Immediately after he died it did not seem enough. The blackness of grief was stark and painful. Could I have said more, done more?

Over the years, however, I have taken comfort in the memory. I have remembered, too, sitting at his bedside stroking the white hairs across his tired head and trying to will him to stay alive only moments before he died. At the time that, too, felt like failure, but today I like to think it eased his passage. I look at Sean's wedding pictures to remember the last hours together as an intact family, not knowing what was to come just a few weeks later. I stare at the last photograph I took of him and my mother standing at the top of the cliff overlooking the October sea, and I look for some sign.

The following year when my wife, Diane, and I were wed, we chose his birthday. I felt as if he were, thus, invited to the occasion. Each year he attends our anniversary. Today he lives on in so many ways. He is still the shadow companion always at my mother's side. He is the father that Sean is now to his children, Ryan and Fiona. He is the gregarious warmth and humor of my younger brother, Nigel. He is the aspiration I always hold to be as kind and gentle as he was.

Memorial Day has passed now for another year, and we have remembered all those fallen in wars, and doubtless those who have left us in whatever way. As Father's Day is upon us, we remember our fathers. For some of us it is a time to look back, for others among whose number I wish I could count myself, it is an opportunity to remember the living.

I shall always be thankful that on an autumn day in 1982, I thought to remember and honor him while he still lived, however imperfectly I expressed it. I shall let it serve to remind me of the importance of knowing and embracing what I have, of having the courage to express it, of giving love while I have the chance.

# INDEPENDENCE DAY
## July 2000

Every few years somebody asks me if we used to celebrate the Fourth of July in England when I was a boy. A raised eyebrow, a quizzical look usually suffices to let the questioner realize the answer for himself. Growing up in England, I recall no mention of the towns of Concord and Lexington in our school history books. Many a schoolboy might have guessed that the fourth of July marked the storming of the Bastille, mistaken, after all, by a mere thirteen years and ten days.

With all the truly American holidays, my lack of childhood history in them deprives me of their full resonance, and I feel somewhat like a New Englander might if he were trying to celebrate Christmas on a beach in Australia on midsummer's day. Of course Thanksgiving has much of the quality of a good old European harvest festival, but since I grew up in the city, that, too, has dwelled solely in my imagination.

Each Patriot's Day my heart goes out to all the English mothers who made their moan, as their red-coated teenage sons perished in battle here. What ancestors of mine might have marched the battle road to Concord and been chased back again under fire? Of what contemporary cousins have I been deprived by the snuffing out of those lives two hundred and twenty-five years ago?

This year on Independence Day, I think about the very word, the very concept. I think about the contradictions. Who, after all, was depending on whom in the 1770s. Being half Irish and half English, I am of the lineage of both oppressor and oppressed, and have never put great store in the achievements of my native country's colonial glory days. So I have no difficulty in rejoicing at the casting off of a yoke, nor in celebrating the hopes and ideals at the birth of a nation, however unfulfilled or incomplete some of those hopes may still seem today.

Divorced from all its political connotations the idea of independence is a complex one. It is, after all, something to which most of us attach great importance. Who, for example, would not wish to be financially independent? Those who have suffered any of a number of physical handicaps often strive mightily for independence.

I like to live in a small town, where I can shop in independent stores rich in character, rather than have to drive the highways in search of a mall. I have spent my whole career proudly associated with independent natural food stores. I value being part of our town, helping to promote individuality, personal service, community responsiveness, rather than feeling lost and faceless in a ghostly corporate entity. What could be better than to be part of a group of people who come together to define and assert their beliefs and values, and give them expression in their daily labor? And there's the rub. For we depend upon each other so!

As children did we not love to finally earn our independence just as soon as we were able, only later to realize just how much we still depended upon our parents in many cases? It's as if we need two words for independence, for we love the freedom to choose, the absence of subordination, the autonomy. The Independent voter is not restricted to his or her party's candidate. The independent country does not have to suffer the exploitation of its colonial parent. But those Minutemen and Minutewomen sure depended on one another.

What a lonely world it would be if there was nobody upon whom I depended. There are those for whom self-employment is the dream. I prefer the mutual contract of employment. A pleasure shared is a pleasure doubled; a burden shared often becomes a pleasure. After twenty-five years in business I continue to enjoy depending upon the contributions, the goodwill, the hard work of so many people. While I know that for so many people being a manager is being caught in the middle, for me, middle child that I am, I would be nowhere else.

And what would marriage be without interdependence? I cannot imagine a life without love, trust, partnership, give and take. I suppose independence seems to me like a step on the road to interdependence; a shaking off of a life of depending without choice; a choosing of those upon whom one wishes to depend, rather than chafing against an enforced yoke; a chance to be depended upon.

So I shall join in the celebration of our glorious Fourth, crowned, ironically, at the Hatch Shell with the work of the great Russian composer Tchaikovsky. I shall remember the ideals of this country's founders, not without questioning both those ideals and the way in which we put them into practice. And when we have celebrated our Independence Day, I shall consider the other 364 days of the year, (or 365 this leap year), as Interdependence Days in which we may celebrate how much we rely upon each other, remember our families, our friends, those closest to us, and appreciate them each day, and ask ourselves how much more we might be doing to approach the goals of liberty and justice and equality.

# PERENNIAL MYSTERIES
## July 2000


One July day a few summers ago Diane and I took a drive
out to Pin Hill Gardens in Harvard, the home of Henry and
Sandy Lefkovits, hybridizers and growers of daylilies. They
had just recovered from the experience of being hosts to a
tour of the American Hemerocallis Society. Their garden was
full as usual with the golden and rosy hues of thousands of
midsummer daylilies, a waving sea of soft sunlit blossoms,
not one of which had been open the previous day; not one of
which would last until tomorrow. Beauty for a day.

So it is with hemerocallis, from the Greek words hemera
meaning day, source also for our word ephemeral, and callis
signifying beauty. The day before the tour, Henry and Sandy
had worked from dawn to dusk removing every single flower,
full or spent, from the stem so that not one spent blossom
should be present for the formal occasion. I can only imagine
their apprehension at looking over the results of their labor by
day's end: a vast expanse of green stems interrupted perhaps
by the slightest blush of an emergent bud. I can also well
imagine their relief to wake the next morning and be greeted
by the whole new incarnation of color.

For most of us who nurture a more modest collection of daylilies, it is easy to look out upon our gardens in the months

of July and August and seem to see the same plants smiling at us with what seem like the same faces each morning. Yet each day is unique, each flower here for one day only. When I come home from work each evening, I try to remember to look at what I know I will have but one chance to see before nightfall steals away with these ephemeral beauties.

Our garden often seems a constant reminder of the paradoxes of life. Each year the wheel turns, perennials emerge from out the once frozen ground, fill us with hope and expectation, rise to their glorious zenith, and fade. As August moves towards September each year I usually feel a sense of melancholy creeping into my being. The vivid greens of early summer are beginning to bleach to more yellowy tones, the loosestrife is filling the wetlands with its purple majesty, afternoon shadows begin to lengthen, darkness draws our evenings a little closer.

With bated breath we await the most splendid time of year. The skies turn azure, the trees remove their veil of chlorophyll to display the red-gold foliage that has lain in wait. The sweet ripeness of the fall harvest fills our nostrils. The crisp cool air enlivens our spirits. The departing geese sing out the final chorus. The curtain falls.

While the garden sleeps under its thick blanket of snow, the wheel turns slowly towards another spring, and for those of us who have wanted to seize the moment and then hang on to it just a little bit longer, there are the photographs. Every summer I click away trying to hold fast to the images of our garden. Like Vita Sackville-West with her famous English garden I sometimes see our plants as my sons and daughters, whose faces will adorn the door of the refrigerator until the next season, the next time in their lives.

One of my favorite daylilies is called 'Yesterday Memories'. I like it for its gentle roseate color as well as for its name. Ephemeral flower that it is, it stands both as a memory of its foregoers and harbinger of tomorrow's flower, which will appear when it is but a memory. On the other side of the garden 'Rachel's Hope' nods its pale apricot-hued agreement.

Beauty for a day, they remind me. In our ever more quickly passing days, all that we most treasure will pass. Our various faiths sustain us in our different understandings of what that means. For me I try to remember that life's greatest sorrows are often the memories of life's greatest joys; that our most profound grief springs from our deepest love. It is a reminder to appreciate the moments that we have.

As one year follows on another, perennials flourish and grow, some die and disappear each winter, but in the spring many return to be divided, some seed their progeny into new and interesting places, others spread themselves aggressively across the border. Clumps of daylilies thicken and flower ever more vigorously. Strong and hardy they survive and thrive from year to year to produce something that is so short-lived, so fragile and delicate.

One of my favorite passages in literature comes from a different Lily. In Virginia Woolf's *To the Lighthouse.* Lily Briscoe, a painter, is trying to realize her vision in a picture she has been working on for many years. "Beautiful and bright it should be on the surface, feathery and evanescent, one colour melting into another like the colours on a butterfly's wings, but beneath the fabric must be clamped together with bolts of iron. It was to be a thing you could ruffle with your breath; and a thing you could not dislodge with a team of horses."

# ORGANIC MONTH IN CONCORD
## September 2000

I was just nineteen years old when I first wondered at the meaning of the term organic. The word arose in an art history class concerning the designs of William Morris, the famous nineteenth-century artist. I was drawn to him, both for his work and because he shared the name Morris with my mother's side of the family, a widespread name in Oxfordshire where I was born. Back in the 1850s he expressed concerns which still ring remarkably true today, warning that much of what is bought and sold "is hurtful to the buyer, more hurtful to the seller, if he only knew." Our houses, he believed, are filled with "tons of unutterable rubbish", the only acceptable things being in the kitchen.

A few years later in 1975, standing over a 35-pound tub of organic crunchy peanut butter, which I was spooning out for a customer in Concord Spice & Grain, I began to learn the meaning of the word as it is so widely used today.

As a child growing up in England, I never thought about our food supply. I believed that I could eat whatever I wanted until the cows come home. I didn't know that one day the cows would come home mad. Finding out about organic and natural foods was a gradual process, an organic process. At first I thought of them primarily in selfish terms. Why would I want to consume foods contaminated with herbicide or pesticide residues, or treated with what we so euphemistically call preservatives?

I must confess that it was not until John Bemis of Hutchin's Farm broadened my consciousness that I understood the true significance of what we were all working for. For it is not simply the harm to me, as an individual consumer of this or that chemical, which should concern me, but rather the environmental damage from years of use of agricultural chemicals which is the greater worry. Looking down the hill from the top of Monument Street to where the farm slopes down to the Concord River just across from the Great Meadows Wildlife Refuge, what could be clearer?

When we purchased our house in Concord, we began to learn about organic lawn care. I like to look out my window and watch the rabbits chewing on clover, the birds wallowing in the birdbath and feeding on the earthworms that live below the soil. Our bio-diverse lawn does require a little weeding from time to time, but it does not build up thatch (micro-organisms digest our clippings), there are no warning signs for neighborhood children after pesticide applications, and we do not live with a high residue carpet indoors from the chemicals that would have been tracked in over the years.

So now as we celebrate Concord's 365th birthday, one trip around the sun for every rotation within each trip, we are asked to consider Concord's legacy and Concord's future, to assemble and say what we think is best about Concord. I am glad that in this old farm town of ours there are many people who care about the environment within and without our boundaries.

I am sure that I would join many creatures in the meadows who are grateful to John and Gordon Bemis for sparing us from over a quarter of a century of chemical run-off. I thank Jim Catterton for promoting organic practices in the community garden plots. I thank Reva and Harold Kasnitz for selling organic foods in our town since the early 1970s at Spice & Grain, and starting me on my personal odyssey. I thank Debra Stark for working so hard to uphold the standards in our industry, and for continuing to bring organic products to Concord. I thank most of all my wife, Diane, for being my companion in this organic journey, both as a partner, sometimes mentor, at Spice & Grain and now as the provider of all the organic meals that nourish me daily. William Morris would, I hope, look favorably upon our kitchen.

These are just the people with whom I have made personal connections, but we all owe thanks to all those whose actions large and small contribute to our daily well-being, for even the consumption of one organic apple is a tiny investment in our future. By the accumulation of small efforts we move forward. Thus, my final thank-you is for Mary Ann Evans, a contemporary of William Morris, better known to us as the author George Eliot, for reminding me of the importance of such small acts, and because I do like a bit of poetry. In her closing words on Dorothea Brooke in the novel *Middlemarch* she writes that "the growing good of the world is partly dependent on unhistoric acts; and that things are not so ill with you and me as they might have been, is half owing to the number who live faithfully a hidden life, and rest in unvisited tombs."

# THANKS FOR THE MEMORIES
## November 2000

Having spent the first twenty-three years of my life in England, I had never heard of Thanksgiving Day until 1975, when I immigrated to Concord. At first it felt to me like a rootless sort of holiday, unanchored by personal memory or history. Its most recognizable tradition, the Thanksgiving turkey, is one in which I have shared but once, having become a vegetarian at the beginning of 1976.

Forsaking this tradition initially gave me a further sense of distance from the celebration. Over the years I have been asked with some frequency what I have for Thanksgiving dinner. As often as not the question has been accompanied by an expression of pity. I am missing out on something. Or am I?

The origins of Thanksgiving are mixed, I believe. Many of us associate it with the pilgrims, whose gratitude for their survival is commemorated with the harvest feast. That first celebration was not, however, the inauguration of an annual event. The first Thanksgiving proclamation was made, it seems, some decades later, setting aside a day in June as the commemorative day. Subsequent proclamations by George Washington more than a hundred years later and by Abraham Lincoln during the Civil War finally established the fourth

Thursday of November as the national day of celebration.

If I think of Thanksgiving as a harvest festival, I feel that as a vegetarian I am all the more wholeheartedly a participant. The vegetarian table which my wife and I share with her family is, indeed, a celebration of the abundant fall harvest, and is lacking in neither variety nor nourishment. Rich in organic beans, squashes, root vegetables, hardy leafy greens and grains, I imagine it has roots that stretch back to ancient feasts such as the Roman Cerelia, honoring the god Ceres, origin of our word cereal.

As a first generation immigrant, I can also imagine that I have a little in common with those first pilgrims, celebrating their adaptation to a new world, albeit that I have been able to travel a considerably smoother path.

Having been so generously embraced by my wife's family these past decades, I have also built up my own fund of personal memories and come to experience the rich familial warmth of the holiday. It is a day to give thanks for a new life built steadily over more than a quarter of a century, to be grateful for the family I have found here through my wife Diane. Within this family which has embraced me, we continually create our own tradition.

As families come together to celebrate, my thoughts also extend to the family I left behind in England. My father died a mere seven years after I moved here. My mother has lived these last decades as a widow, while I and my brothers Sean and Nigel have all advanced into our middle age. As we move inexorably forward we gather evermore the rich harvest of our lives, celebrating the melancholy joy of a rich past and a diminishing future.

I can still remember the first time that I stopped and wondered that my brothers loved me. I was nine years old, returning from the hospital in the dawn of a spring morning, having fallen out of bed and broken my collar bone in the night. When my father brought me back into the house, I saw their tear-stained faces as they sat at the head of the stairs outside our bedroom door. It was one of those rare moments when, as a child I stopped to notice and fully appreciate the bond between us.

I remember my very first day of school a few years earlier, crying at the classroom window, as I saw Sean playing outside in the rain, from which we newcomers were held back. I recall what felt like the last summer of my childhood, at fourteen years of age, playing on the floor day after day with eleven-year-old Nigel, sensing that this was an ending.

I remember flying back to the United States after the first time that I returned to England in 1979, feeling my heart threatening to break at what I had left without really saying good-bye to until then. Over the years I have found that that

45

absence has not so much made my heart grow fonder as it has made my awareness keener.

The only Thanksgiving Day that I spent with my brothers was in 1982, the week after my father died. I waited to return to this country until the following day, not having the heart for festivity that year. But now even that goes into the storehouse of memories alongside the moments both painful or precious. Often both.

The rich granaries of experience, as the author and psychotherapist Viktor Frankl puts it, give shape and meaning to our lives. As the year draws to a close and the darkness begins to form about us, may we remember each other, stop and absorb the fullness of present moments, and give thanks for our full harvest of memories.

# TRAVELLERS ALL
## February 2001

The rising sun streamed in through the back window of the car as I headed west on Route 2 a few weeks ago on my way to work. Ahead in the opposite sky I watched the full Wolf Moon of February simultaneously sliding towards the snowy western horizon.

The last time I was paying sufficient attention to observe this phenomenon of moon and sun rising and setting in opposite skies was last October. I was in Boston with an hour to spend before meeting Diane to come home to Concord. Perhaps when I was younger I would have thought of it as an hour to kill. At this time in my life, and on this occasion, I thought of it as an hour to savor.

It was the balmy evening of an Indian Summer day, and being one of the legion of mid-life men with back problems, I decided to drive over to Castle Island, lie on the beach and perform my all-important back exercises under the warming glow of the sunset.

I parked the car in the lot and wended my way to a remote spot where I thought my performance would be as inconspicuous as possible. Stretched out with my back pressed firmly into the warm and gravelly sand, my feet pointed back across the bay towards the Boston skyline, I waved, lifted, rotated and otherwise extended my limbs in various therapeutic ways, then rested a moment as I prepared to do the sit-ups.

Unconsciously I had positioned myself so perfectly, legs bent and slightly apart, that when I pulled my upper body up from the ground I was greeted by the setting sun framed precisely between my knees. The warm earth supporting me, the solar glow on my face, the unexpected serendipity of this moment took my breath away. I lingered until the sun slipped behind the buildings of South Boston.

I was still basking in some feeling of connectedness when I rose to make my way back towards the car and into town. Turning round from the bay, I saw the calm waters of Boston Harbor stretching out towards the open ocean, and in the eastern sky the full moon rising. The Hunter's Moon, I believe it must have been, which lingers like the Harvest Moon in our equinoctial sky, giving a welcome extra light to hunters or farmers, whichever the case may be, in the waning days of summer.

Overhead the glint of an underbelly of a plane flashed as it sped westward chasing the sunset. Most of the flights to Europe were also preparing to cross the Atlantic where they would in a few hours be speeding into an accelerating sunrise, carrying their passengers across space and time. Earlier in the summer Diane and I had stood on the island and watched one of the last of the tall ships gliding past us as it carried its crew of sailors young and old on a voyage across the seas. Riding on the tide pulled by this moon of ours, it slipped out beyond the outer harbor as we stood and watched and waved. The ground, so firm beneath our feet, all the while rotated, revolved, and hurtled through space in continuation of its flight from the Big Bang.

So last month, watching the moon set as the sun climbed behind me, I was struck by the sensation of symmetry: winter framed between these personal celestial observations. Our New England winter, such as we had not seen in a few years, is beginning to loose its grip, even if it is still occasionally able to muster a few sharp blasts before departing. Our ice dams have melted and finally drained away in the warmth of a late February thaw. The ground, which we have not seen since before the dark days of solstice, has peeked out, if only briefly, from beneath its snowy cover. Even a March blizzard lacks the tenacity of midwinter snows and freezes.

This week's full moon will once again be an equinoctial moon, as we will have passed almost halfway round the sun since that October day. The light of early March is now equal to the light of October, although the balmy warmth is yet awhile off. We have already looked out of our front window hoping to see the first snowdrop heralding oncoming spring. In the suntrap under our front porch the first tips of iris reticulata have broken though the ground. Invisible under the snow beneath the linden tree, crocuses are forcing their way upward. The groundhog's shadow is shortening.

The 130th New England Spring Flower Show beckons in a matter of weeks. Even in the dark interior of a Boston exposition center, the feel of grass blades between one's fingers, the scent of rhododendron and azalea, the bright bursts of color which dance before eyes hungry from winter's greyness will pull us round the circle as we move from season to season, moon to moon, sunrise to sunrise; one year, one month, one day, one moment at a time.

# BENEATH THE DREAMING SPIRES
## April 2001

There is no place in the world that affects me in quite the way that Oxford does. The city of dreaming spires where I was born and spent the first twelve years of my life seems always like a mirage to me now when I visit.

Nestled in the Thames valley, just east of England's Cotswold Hills, Oxford greeted us on this day with sunshine. My mother, my younger brother Nigel and his wife Karen are visitors for the day in a city filled with history and with personal memories.

As we drive through the center, the 16th century Gothic buildings of the University continue to draw today's students through their portals to green grass quadrangles and quiet cloistered rooms. The city around them bustles with its cosmopolitan blend of scholars, tourists, natives moving between the old examination rooms on High Street, the long standing Blackwell's bookstore on Broad Street or the more recent Starbucks coffee shop just around the corner from one of Oxford's most famous landmarks, the 18th century domed Radcliffe Camera.

Long Wall Street, which carries the old soot-stained city wall around the colleges, winds its way complete with 21st century speed bumps, delivering us to the Sheldonian Theater with its carved pillars of the twelve apostles. Students stroll beneath the Bridge of Sighs arching across a narrow side street.

Childhood memories seem strangely distorted by the changes which have been subtly or not so subtly wrought by the intervening forty years. Brightly colored vehicles, video rental shops, modern coffee bars interrupt my memory of bicycles, boxy black motor-cars and dark red double-decker buses.

A mile or two beyond the center lies Cowley, where my father worked at Morris and Beecham's, my grandfather's coal merchant office, and where I and my two brothers attended school in the 50's and early 60's.

Pressed Steel, where my father first came to work as an Irish immigrant during the Second World War is long gone, a remnant of the clock tower alone still standing as a memorial. Morris Motors, founded by one of Oxfordshire's multitude of Morrises (Morris Dancing, Inspector Morse, my Granddad Dick Morris) is also gone. Holloway, the road that ran between the factory gates, still leads towards Headington and the house in which I was conceived and born. Driving through today, I remember every noontime, after coming to Dad's office from school, he would take us home for lunch, or dinner as we called it then. We would try to pass the factory gates before the whistle blew to discharge a thousand men on bicycles likewise wheeling home for their midday dinner, and causing Dad to curse if we were stuck behind them.

Farther along we pass the barracks, where I earned the singular distinction of being the only person I ever knew who took a wrong turn in a 440 yard race on the track in the qualifier for school sports day.

In Headington we pass the recreation ground where the old gray-steel wooden-seated swings and roundabout have been replaced by more vividly painted plastic-coated versions of the same, and turn into Quarry High Street. The sprawling lilac still stands before what was once our little red brick family home. Nigel and I walk down Coppock's alley, an unnamed path between the houses in the 50's. Peering across the low garden walls which towered over our heads back then, we see the back of the Atwells' house, where little Steven used to crouch behind his wall throwing stones across at us, and ducking to avoid our missiles coming back, while old Mrs. Taylor occupied the no man's land between, shaking her fist from her rear window.

At the back of the house I walk into the parking area for the development that was built shortly before we left. The crumbling cotswold-stone wall still separates our properties. From the other side of the wall, I reach over into our former garden and touch the laurel tree that I helped my father plant in 1959. A tiny shrub back then, it now obscures the remodeled back of the old house. Carefully, I pluck off one shiny leaf to carry away with me, something living from a long distant past.

We go to visit my Aunt Gretta and Uncle Kevin, who, in addition to my cousin Don and his family, are the sole remaining relatives in the town, living half a mile from the now disused Littlemore railway station where my grandfather still received coal until the early 1960's, and where Sean and I would sometimes stand beside him in the makeshift office watching the soot-faced coalmen loading up their trucks for the day's deliveries

Everywhere I look I see strangers. In the faces of passers-by, I search for a familiar now grown school friend, but it is as if they are all gone, as if the world of my childhood has passed out of existence, the city living on depopulated of the all the familiar faces of my past, replacing them with strangers, and leaving behind the small child inside myself holding fast to the memories and searching for their meaning.

I little knew in those days that one of the customers at Berry's bakery in Headington, Jim McColl, whom I may have even stood beside, when we made one of our daily after-school stops there, would be met many years later in my new hometown of Concord; that as I played in Coppock's Alley, one of the students at the University at that time, Tom Sisson, would become a friend and neighbor here on Sudbury Road, and that the University would soon have a chef from Avignon named Robert Didier, who would also appear in Concord at La Provence on Thoreau Street.

As I write this, the leathery green laurel leaf beside me on the desk is already advancing towards the brown and dessicated state which will be its fate. Just as the tree lives on in our former back garden, so too does all this past live on inside me, growing, changing, mutating as memory, imagination and experience cast their spell. Perhaps in another two years when I return for my biennial pilgrimage, I will be able to reach a little higher up the tree and once more pluck off a new leaf.

# A CHILD'S CHRISTMAS IN ENGLAND
## December 2002

"One Christmas was so much like another in those years..."
*A Child's Christmas in Wales* by Dylan Thomas has become
a fond tradition for me in the 27 years that I have lived in
Concord, attempting for myself to recall the lost world of a
receding childhood romanticized by selective memory and an
ever-present love for the family that we once were. My father,
grandparents, uncles, aunts, "alas no longer whinnying with
us," yet live on in the remembrance of Christmases past.

In the 1950's and 60's we spent Christmas every year at my
grandparents. They had founded a small club on the out-
skirts of Oxford. Temple Farm Country Club they called
it. The oldest part of the building dated back to the twelfth
century, and during the reformation it had served as a secret
monastery.

Every year family and friends gathered to celebrate at their
table. My two brothers and I looked forward to the Christmas presents, some surprises, others secrets which Granddad
had been unable to keep despite Gran's admonitions. While
the adults indulged in a little Christmas spirit at the bar, we
waited for our uncles and aunts, some by blood, some simply

by deference and familiarity, to shower us with gifts. Amidst the fulfilled hope of toys and the disappointment of socks, we absorbed the atmosphere of the season.

If we had stayed over Christmas Eve we were still sleepy from the excitement of having been up until midnight to receive the first gifts from our grandparents. We slept upstairs in a guest room, wondering whether we would hear the gray lady who haunted the hallways, or if anyone would see the coach full of headless monkeys that came up the driveway after midnight, and if the driver looked at you, you would die within the year.

Christmas dinner started at about two o'clock after the regular patrons had left the premises to the inner circle of relatives and friends. Sitting around the table with our gaily colored paper hats, after reading the jokes and inspecting the tiny toys from our pulled crackers, trying to get the miniature ball into the miniature cup to which it was attached by a string, we ate our way through all the yuletide fare, which was topped by Christmas Pudding.

It is the Christmas Pudding tradition which has stayed with me. A few years ago I decided to bring back at least one vestige from that distant past and looked up a Christmas Pudding recipe. Not surprisingly it was full of things which I now foreswear. Sugar, white flour, lard, ale, liquor. "I bet one can make it with entirely healthy ingredients," I said to myself. Fifteen years later I have enjoyed many years of serving this recipe to family and friends, who have all delighted in this flavor of old England. Both the uninitiated and the experienced have wondered at the fragrance and flavor. I'm sure the recipe has undergone many changes. I never follow it exactly, but it always comes out perfectly. The following recipe makes one large and two small puddings.

## TRADITIONAL ENGLISH CHRISTMAS PUDDING
### Ingredients

$3/_4$ cup wholewheat pastry flour

1 teaspoon baking powder

1 $1/_2$ teaspoons cinnamon

$1/_3$ teaspoon ground cloves

$1/_3$ teaspoon ground ginger

$1/_3$ teaspoon ground nutmeg

8 oz. coconut oil

8 oz. dry breadcrumbs

grated rind and juice of one lemon

8 oz. Sucanat or Rapadura (unrefined brown sugar)

4 oz. chopped pecans

12 oz. raisins

8 oz. date pieces

8 oz. chopped figs

1 $1/_2$ cups apple juice

1 $1/_2$ cups milk or soy milk

## Directions

Mix first six (dry) ingredients. Add coconut oil, breadcrumbs, lemon rind, sugar, nuts and fruits. Mix thoroughly. Make a well and add lemon juice, apple juice and milk. Mix thoroughly. Cover with cloth and store overnight in refrigerator.

On the following day, stir and moisten if necessary. (I never have). Fill well-greased pudding basin to within one inch of the top, cover with pleated greaseproof paper (wax paper), and tie tightly. (I use a rubber band). Place on a trivet (small wire rack) in a large covered pot or pressure cooker of boiling water. The water should come one half to three quarters of the way up the pudding basin. Steam for four hours (three if you use a pressure cooker), checking and refilling water level as necessary. I burned this pudding twice by failing to do so.

I have served this both right away or a few days later, in which case I just wrap it in greaseproof paper and refrigerate it, then re-steam it for 45 minutes before serving. My favorite accompaniment is plain cream, organic of course, poured over it. Then I close my eyes and think of England.

# DANDELION DAYS
## April 2004

Mowing the lawn for the first time this year, I see the dandelions awakening to Spring. As organic gardeners, Diane and I tolerate, often embrace, the diversity of greens that appear throughout our lawn. Violets, purple and white varieties, are scattered here and there across the backyard. Our little crop of scilla multiplying year by year beneath the linden tree has already come and gone. Clover will add nitrogen to our soil all summer.

The dandelions we tolerate more briefly. Each year they return; each year we dig them out with our trusty dandelion diggers. It usually takes about four trips around the property in the course of a week or so, and then their season, too, is passed. But as their defiant faces greet us again after each digging and from year to year, I think of my grandmother and enjoy them. The dandelion was her favorite flower.

Gran was born in England in the Spring of 1902. With her father in the navy and her mother employed in a children's home in London, she was brought up largely by her Grannie and her Uncle Harold, who kept a public house called The Peacock in Oxford. At night she watched from her bedroom window as fights, sometimes with drawn knives, broke out in the street below. Her best friends during her childhood were the tramps who regularly passed through the doss house that was attached to her uncle's pub. Her Uncle Harold taught her to shoot in his shooting gallery and won many bets on her marksmanship. She came to be known as the little Annie Oakley.

She lived through World War I as a teenager, married my grandfather in 1923 and went through World War II as the mother of two teenagers.

She was nearing sixty by the time I have any fixed memory of her. I never saw her as the young beauty who was asked to sit as an artist's model, but that beauty lived in her face until her last days in her nineties. It was not the beauty of cultivation, but something natural and wild, tempered by a life of some hardship. As a teenager she had heard herself described by one of Oxford University's elite young men who frequented her uncle's pub as an "orchid bud in a cesspool."

Mostly I remember her for her resilience. Her life's experience taught her that succumbing to or even exhibiting emotion was a weakness. I do not recall her ever being sick. She did not believe in doctors. Hard work was her therapy.

When we were children it was Granddad that we loved. We loved him for his childlike playfulness, his mischief, his whisky-breathed storytelling, his inability to keep the secret of our Christmas gifts: the ones that Gran had bought. I had to grow up to understand the depth of her love. I never saw her cry, but I often recall her with her chin set, quivering slightly, a mist behind her eyes.

After Granddad died at 67, she continued to work full-time until she was 83. When she was finally forced to retire, she lived beside the sea, where I would visit on trips to England. She made her last visit here when she was 88. The last time I saw her was on the occasion of my mother's (her daughter's) 70th birthday. In the restaurant the staff thought she must be the 70-year-old. When we said goodbye, I sensed that she believed it would be a last farewell. The chin and eyes told me. A few months later in the Spring of 1995, shortly after her 93rd birthday she went to bed one evening and did not wake the next morning. She was buried amongst the dandelions.

Shortly before she was ninety years old, she had asked me to transcribe some of her memoirs. Remembering a childhood whose hardships were mollified by the love of her own grandmother, she wrote, "I was so very lucky to have had these experiences...for they taught me so much. Tolerance above all, which I think is the most vital of all other things; love, kindness, thoughtfulness and forgiveness."

# DEPARTURES
## June 2004

I watched my mother pass through the gate to board the British Airways plane that would carry her across the 31 million square miles of ocean that separate our homes. Turning around, I walked back dully into this vast North American continent that has been my home for almost thirty years. In all those years the good-byes have not become any easier.

The departure lounge of an airport has always been a place of grief for me. Now, saying goodbye yet one more time, all the accumulated sorrows of the years crowded in on me. The last time I saw my father on his feet was in 1982 at Heathrow Airport. Two months later he had died, and I had just enough time to reach his bedside for his final hours. We never know when we will say our final good-byes, but as an expatriate I imagine some of mine will be concealed in airport farewells.

Logan Airport is full of memories for me, and even now, as the international terminal is changed beyond recognition, the memories remain fully intact. There are the happy memories of arrivals: I spent most of my thirtieth birthday at Logan Airport waiting for my brother Sean and his fiancée Viv to arrive on a flight that was twice diverted. The first time my parents came here in 1978 my mother was only the age that I am now. When they left after two weeks I realized for the first time the magnitude of the loss it was for me to have torn myself from my roots. When I left England to travel I had been too young, too desirous of my independence, to know how much I loved them. Now I realized that I would be able to count the number of times I would see them again in my life. I realized, too, that I had said good-bye to my childhood, to a part of myself. I had crashed into reality. As my brothers have come and gone over the years, tear-choked good-byes at airports have become a feature of my life; every farewell foreshadowing that final parting.

As the roots that I have established here in Concord have become stronger year by year, happily married to Diane, tending our own home and garden, welcomed into her family, working in a community store where there is a strong sense of belonging, the recoveries have become quicker. But at each moment of parting the intensity of sorrow carries all the force of the years.

Driving the four-lane highway back to Concord under the bright blue New England sky, I feel adrift in a strange and foreign country. Roadside daylilies blaze with today's bright orange glory even as yesterday's blooms wither on the stalk. The camera on the seat beside me holds the images of our spent vacation.

All the years seemed to have passed by as relentlessly as the trees that are streaking past the car window. Did my mother

ever imagine she would one day have three gray-haired sons?
Memories flood my being.

When I was a small boy my family moved a hundred miles
from Oxford to Bournemouth. I still remember my Grandmother's quivering chin and mist-filled eyes as she waved to
us from her driveway. I remember four years later the shock
and tears at my Grandfather's funeral in 1967, when his coffin was carried into the church to the strains of *Onward
Christian Soldiers*. I remember the November morning in
1982 watching my mother lay down quietly on the hospital
bed beside my father for one last time. I remember Dad's last
gasp of breath two hours later, as we all reached for him.

I am now almost at the age Mum was when she was widowed. Mum is the last of her generation left. Her brother
died in 1995. My father's brothers and sisters are all gone.
My youngest brother Nigel will be fifty next year. My grandniece will be looking for her driver's license next year.

Seeing each other once a year or sometimes less frequently,
we do not take each other for granted. This seems to be sorrow's reward, reminding us to love before we lose. Life is a
short story with a sad ending. Knowing that is hard. Airport
farewells force me to accept the sadness. They also remind
me to embrace our fleeting joys.

# THE LAST MOWS OF SUMMER
## October 2004

In the long shadows of an autumnal evening, walking behind my lawn mower, I hear the sound of other motors echoing the call from across the neighborhood. Grass that was once long and lush and turgid is now drier, thinner, beginning to turn towards its winter dormancy. The stripes from last week's cut are still visible as the growth begins to slow.

The year for me often seems easily divided into two seasons: six months of growth and six months of sleep. Lawn mowing begins in the middle of April and ends in the middle of October, precisely half of a year. Summer may officially begin in June and end in September, but days of summer are often sprinkled liberally throughout the growing time. Having grown up in England, I still find that a seventy-degree day epitomizes summer.

But even as I conceive the season to its fullest possible length, it seems too short already. Was it not just a few weeks ago that the daffodils first made their appearance? Throughout the winter Diane and I nurtured bulbs in pots, moving them from basement to garage to breezeway; in and out, up and down as temperatures demanded. In April we were rewarded with a celebration of both soft and vivid colors. 'February

Gold' came first (obviously given its name in a warmer zone than ours.) Then 'Pipit', 'Quail', 'Sweetness'. Soon they were joined by daffodils in the landscape, transporting us from winter into spring: 'Ice Follies', 'Ice Wings', 'Papillon Blanc', and 'Bridal Crown'.

Tulips came in May, and leaves on trees. Nepeta and lady's mantle graced the border. In June our single peony plant put forth its luxuriant pinks, and this year for once it did not rain on the following day to turn the flowers to mush, as it seems to have done for the last ten years. Heavy rain on the tenth of June had seemed a guarantee until now.

Summer's zenith always seems to me to be the daylily season. Strong and sturdy and floriferous our plants thrive in their sunny spot. The blooms seem so exuberant and full of substance, and yet each day they bloom and die. From day to day one bloom will give way to the next. 'Gentle Rose', 'Happy Returns', 'Second Thoughts', 'Yesterday Memories'. They come and they go, and lead us into August, the browning of late summer. Joy and melancholy are intertwined. The golds and purples and magentas of rudbeckias and echinaceas and loosestrife seem to harbinger the blaze of glory in which the season will soon end.

September brings us the rich maroons of sedum and eupatorium, the purple asters and chrysanthemums, and now I watch and await the final days, when stripped of chlorophyll our shrubs and trees show us their true colors, saving the best for last. Gold and scarlet in front of an azure sky. The fall harvest of apples and squash ripens and matures.

Below the ground daffodils begin to send their roots down into the dark earth. Within each bulb a perfect tiny flower has already formed, to be held throughout the cold months, suspended, until the return of the first warm days gives the signal to begin their re-emergence.

Following the lawnmower through the lengthening shadows, I remember summers past. Standing on my father's hands as he lifted me high above the lawn of our back garden. Bouncing down the garden path on pogo sticks with my brothers. Was I not like a flower in a bulb then, my small self ready to emerge into all the life ahead of me? I remember my first day of school looking for my brother from the window of a new classroom as the rain kept us indoors. Leaving for college on a late September day. Arriving in this country nearly thirty years ago. Twenty years in this house and garden.

There is still some growing season ahead of us. My friend Ray will still be picking his organic vegetable crop at Applefield Farm in Stow until November, before he comes to join us indoors, cooking at the Natural Gourmet for the winter. Then we will celebrate Thanksgiving, and as the darkness falls around us, Diane and I will pot up a few more bulbs to nurture in readiness and hope.

# IN THE DEEP MIDWINTER
## January 2005

Some moments are not so easy to live in. As I stare at the screen of my computer, I know that outside the window behind my back, and all around me, the snow is beginning to accumulate quickly. I have just driven home rumbling through the dusky snow-enclosed world between Maynard and Concord.

All the way the car's headlights illuminated sparkling jewel-like flecks dancing like a swarm of frozen fireflies in silent midwinter revelry. Evergreens began to fill their outstretched limbs with falling snow. Enfolded in winter's still beauty, I rolled slowly into the driveway and trod across the squeaking snow to the front door.

Now back inside I think about the snow shovel, calculate how many times and at what intervals I should go out in order to keep up with the expected snowfall. I spent this morning thawing out the frozen-solid sump pump hose and reassembling it in hopes of keeping the floods from last week from invading the basement.

The newsman tells us that power outages are possible. The temperature has not been within twenty degrees of freezing for two days. The magic moments of winter, the warmth of home amidst the blizzard cannot quite keep the worm of worry at bay, and I find myself wishing for spring.

Downstairs in the basement fifteen pots of daffodils and assorted spring bulbs wait beneath a window which we open and close, open and close all season long trying to maintain the required temperature for them to have their needed winter. Their roots gradually creep down through the soil as we nurture them towards their emergence. Last year we did this for the first time, monitoring their temperature with a remote thermometer, watching over them, sometimes going down in the middle of the night to close the window if we were afraid the nearby water-pipes might freeze, or to open it if their microclimate warmed too much.

On warmer days in February, and in March especially, we will carry them upstairs and put them outdoors for the day. At dusk we will carry them back down. Over time they will migrate day by day, hour by hour from basement to porch to garage, in and out, up and down. All the while they will continue to make themselves ready. The tiny perfectly-formed flower presently enclosed inside the bulb will have its two or three weeks of glory and then fade.

Planting daffodils over the last few years, I have come to appreciate the vast number of forms and colors of narcissus. From the ruffled split corona of 'Parisienne', sumptuous as a Georgia O'Keeffe painting, to the almost peony-like double

'Bridal Crown', there are pinks and reds, golds and yellows, brilliant whites and creams. There are large cups and small, multi-flowering tazettas, miniatures, bi-colors and reverse bi-colors, trumpets and starbursts.

While perennialized daffodils in our garden beds sleep beneath their blanket of white with no mind for discontent, I am assailed by hopes and fears, expectations and worries, desire and loss, dreams and memories. As the finely pow-dered diamonds swirl outside, I knead the muscles of my lower back in preparation for the shovel.

The attempt to appreciate each moment meets with greater or lesser success at every moment. The older I become, the less willing I am to seek to skip forward to the next week, the next season, the next year, wishing my life away. Liv-ing in the unwonted prosperity of this place at this time in this world, it often seems that my worries mostly amount to fears of having this silver spoon removed from my mouth, but being human I do keep a firm bite on it at times.

I remind myself: I have a house to worry about; I have heat to be afraid of losing. I pull myself into this present, this gift.

Maybe tomorrow or the next day if the sun returns I will take some of those deep-blue-sky and crystalline-snow pho-tographs to produce next year's Christmas card. Celebrating, even memorializing this moment, I shall walk slowly towards the coming spring. I will still be excited to see the first snow-drops appearing beneath the linden tree. I will cheer on our potted daffodils when they finally break through the surface and come into amazing and varied flower on our doorstep.

When their season is at its height I shall have to resist the temptation to worry about spring rains and floods and whatever else my mind might try to fix on. And as the fragrant scent of narcissus fills the air, first herald of the seasons yet to follow, I will remind myself to wait patiently to smell the roses.

# SURE A LITTLE BIT OF HEAVEN
## March 2005

Everyone who knows me identifies me as an Englishman. But for at least one day of the year I celebrate the other half of my heritage. My father was born in Cork, Ireland in 1916, and came to England in the 1940's to help the war effort. He met my mother in Oxford, where they settled and had their three sons. I was named after his father, James Leahy.

As a boy I first thought of myself as English. I always knew that my Dad and half of my relatives were foreigners. There was music in the way they spoke; they began sentences with the word "sure"; they sang plaintive songs about the old country and their mother.

By the time I started school I was proud to be half-Irish. I could make the sign of the cross speaking Gaelic, and could also ask you to pass the salt. I also knew that I was the heir to the kings of Ireland. Being princes didn't really set me and my brothers apart, even when Dad said we were always leaders.

Sometimes before bedtime when Dad would sit me down and sing, whiskey-breathed and misty-eyed, about the little bit of Heaven that fell from out the sky one day, I, too, could close my eyes and wish to be back in our lost kingdom. When I was nine years old, I brought two boys home from the playground, because they would not believe that I was the son of a prince. Dad was washing our little car in the driveway, when I asked him to explain to them. He said something about history and things not being that simple, and a different country, and when they left I knew I would never brag about that again.

When we moved to Bournemouth in 1964, I started at a new school. I told a friend of mine that the Irish form of James is Seamus. This became my name until I left in 1970. Sometimes I was proud of it, but when the thick-headed Irishman so often cropped up in jokes by the name of Paddy or Seamus, I could less easily embrace the name, which my schoolmates had given to me as a joke to begin with. When I started college I chose my own name, Jim.

I did not visit Ireland until 1984, eighteen months after my father died. It was a pilgrimage of sorts, accompanied by my mother, my brother Sean and his wife Viv. Dad never returned there after 1949. All but one of his brothers and sisters emigrated eventually, ending up in England or the United States.

When we were young children Dad had always talked about going back to Ireland, but in the 1950's and 60's it was a long distance to travel and a lot of money. Sometimes we used to wonder if he was afraid that it would break his heart to see it once again.

Being in Cork in 1984 I looked for him everywhere. We went to the house where he was born on Western Road, visited the site of the old Opera House where he had performed so often as a professional comedian. We strolled along Patrick Street ("Pana" to the locals), where Dad could never walk without stopping to talk, at length no doubt, with the many friends he would meet there. We drove past Tivoli, the house on the harbor where his sister Dolly and her husband Jack had stood on the balcony waving their enormous white tablecloth as my parents sailed into town for their honeymoon in 1949. We passed a street called Sunday's Well, and I remembered the middle-aged priest who had turned up in Bournemouth just a few years before. Dad was introduced to him after mass. "Jesus, sure you're Tom Wiseman from Sunday's Well," he exclaimed. "You're Dick Leahy from the Wesy Road!" the priest replied. And each of them saw in that moment the little boy in the school uniform, sideways cap and satchel swinging.

Now each of these memories recedes layer upon layer to be pulled out and re-examined each year on St. Patrick's Day. I have always been more of an internationalist than a patriot. I've never quite related to waving the flag, perhaps because the flag of the country where I was born was for so long the symbol of oppression in my father's homeland. I still cheer for England when the World Cup comes round every four years, and in the middle of March I always try to wear something green, eat Irish soda bread, listen to those plaintive airs which speak to me as they might to any immigrants who have left their homeland, their roots and their family.

In my closet I keep a small lapel pin of the Irish flag, which Dad once gave me, and every March 17th I pull it out to wear for a day. It serves not so much to remind me of my Irishness, but to remind me that in my heart I am always the son of a prince.

# ARE WE THERE YET?
## March 2005

When I was seven years old, we would pack up each summer for our two-week vacation in Bournemouth. My father, mother and two brothers would all pile into our little Morris Minor and set off on the ninety-mile drive from Oxford to our favorite coastal resort. Wending our way through the winding roads of the English countryside, we would pass through small rural villages and, spaced almost equidistantly, the larger towns of Newbury, Andover and Salisbury. Somewhere between the towns of Newbury and Andover the plaintive sounds of "Where are we?" would begin to emanate from our backseat. From Salisbury until we reached our destination, it might be replaced by the periodic whine: "Are we there yet?"

At the age of about fourteen, by which time we had actually moved to Bournemouth, and had some years since discarded the fantasy that we would be on permanent vacation there, I was given an essay assignment titled "It is better to travel than to arrive."

My young adolescent mind could not comprehend the wider philosophical question, and I proceeded to write a labored, unimaginative story about cars and trains and travel sickness. One boy alone grasped the possibilities and addressed the concept of whether anticipation might not often be more pleasurable than fulfillment. Perhaps he had read some of Shakespeare's sonnets, his admonition to the lovelorn -- "before, a joy proposed; behind, a dream", or maybe his parents had simply given him a clue. At the age of fourteen I was a student of Latin, but had not yet come across the phrase "carpe diem", let alone stopped to entertain such a notion.

Now as we move into spring, I find myself asking with the same childish impatience of the seven-year old: "Are we there yet?" Meteorological spring began a month ago; the equinox has come and gone. But March has certainly had its leonine moments, leaving most of us wondering when we will be saying goodbye to winter. As April begins we are surely hoping that it will not be "the cruelest month."

At home, our attempt to bring some spring to our winter took the form of fifteen pots of daffodils, hyacinths, and tulips forced for early bloom. Even as the snow continued to assail us, our pots of colorful blooms filled our plant window with hope, and were taken outdoors on daily excursions to decorate our front doorstep.

At the New England Spring Flower Show just passed, impatient gardeners tried to cast off the gloom of the departing season amidst an extravaganza of whole seasons of flowers concentrated into one exhibition. Harbingers of spring and summer abounded as daffodils and delphiniums (unlikely bedfellows) bloomed together even while a Nor'easter raged outside.

Today as I walk through the back yard, I see that the snow-drop, which showed its first bloom weeks ago only to be buried under white, has re-emerged beneath one of our linden trees. Under another, crocuses are making their way up. In the garden bed, 'Ice Follies', perhaps nature's most vigorous daffodils, are coming back for their seventh season. Bulbs which we had forced last year and then given to the compost pile are poking their heads out from under the arbor vitae trimmings. 'Monte Carlo' tulips are beginning to show beneath the bay window. In a more subtle reminder of months still further off, daylily greens are peeking out from the soil by the front step, and as we pull back last fall's ground-up leaves, with which we mulched our beds, the first ruffs of Sedum 'Autumn Joy' are visible beneath.

But let's not think of autumn just yet. If we have lost our patience with winter, perhaps we will be restored by spring. We may all remember some good snowstorms in April and even one May surprise about twenty-five years ago, but it does seem that we are finally there. The grass will soon be taking on its lush green hue. The buds will start to break on the forsythia. Milder temperatures will draw us outside. As I sweep away the sand pushed up onto the lawn by the snowplows, I will see all the signs of growth around me, and when the spring flowers burst into glorious bloom, I will try to drink in all I can of the fleeting moment, knowing that even though we are finally there now, it is not our destination, for still we travel on.

# DANCING WITH THE DAFFODILS
## April 2005

Diane and I first took an interest in daffodils about six years ago. In the fall of 1999, while most of us were worrying about the Y2K problem, we decided that one antidote would be to plant daffodils for the new millennium. We did not expect to advance the cause of world peace with this gesture (we would certainly have been disappointed if we had), but it did seem to offer some alternative to fear of the abyss with which the world of technology seemed to be threatening us.

I think if you had asked me at that time to describe a daffodil, I would have expressed what is probably most people's concept of a small yellow trumpet-shaped flower which appears in spring. When we planted 200 bulbs of 'Ice Follies' (white with a yellow cup), 'Accent' and 'Salome' (white with a pink cup), and 'Mount Hood' (all white), I began to see the limitations of my perception.

My eyes were truly opened, however, when we attended the Seven States Daffodil Show at Tower Hill Botanical Gardens in April, 2001. We were there not just because of our personal enthusiasm for daffodils, but because in the fall of 2000, Diane had signed up to prepare a presentation on daffodils for the horticulture study group of the Acton Garden

Club, of which she was a member. Attending the show was part of the study. For me it was also an assignment, as Diane had asked me if I would be willing to take some slides to accompany her presentation.

Perhaps if I had not been focusing my attention through the lens of a camera, I would not have been so amazed by the varieties of form and color which met my eye. In the exhibition room little glass vases of perfectly formed flowers competed for the judges' awards. I learned that there were thirteen divisions of Narcissus, each with its own separate characteristics. There were large trumpets in a fanfare of colors, small disc-like cups of reds and oranges, luxurious doubles, some more closely resembling multi-colored peonies than my conception of a daffodil. There were frilly split coronas like 'Parisienne' with all the sumptuous beauty of an iris. There were miniatures smaller than a fingernail, fragrant jonquils with their reed-like stems, the tiny hoop-petticoat-styled bulbocodium (all trumpet and insignificant perianth petals).

Outside in the gardens we were taken on a tour with David Burdick, a Western Massachusetts daffodil grower. As he led the group through the gardens, he indulged me as I explained why I was kneeling, stooping, sometimes crawling through the plantings to record on film the beauty of spring bursting out from beneath brown leaves, gray twigs and otherwise barren surroundings. We saw starbursts in the Entry Garden, brilliant white poeticus in the Lawn Garden, frizzy 'Rip

Van Winkle' under a pine tree, golden 'Saint Patrick's Day' and the reverse bi-color 'Spellbinder' in the Secret Garden. We saw floriferous 'Silver Chimes' tazettas and 'Fruit Cup' jonquils in the Orangerie.

We finished up in the Systematic Garden, one of the more recently developed areas at Tower Hill, where plants are displayed in beds according to their families. Along the left border each of the thirteen divisions of Narcissus was assigned its space, so that one could walk along the border and compare each variety with the next, or stand back and see the abundant varieties in one harmonious kaleidoscope.

Four years later, Diane has given her presentation both to the Acton Garden Club and last spring to the Garden Club Federation of Massachusetts Horticulture Study Group. Last September, Janet Richards, a designer and artist in Acton, partnered Diane in the creation of an educational exhibit which appeared in a flower show at the Acton Library.

Now the Daffodil Show at Tower Hill is upon us once more. This year we go as participants as well as observers. Diane and Janet's educational exhibit will stand proudly in the foyer. The slide show, which has been refined and expanded over the years, will be shown at one o'clock on Sunday. After four years I finally get the pleasure of publicly presenting these pictures myself. Tower Hill is just a few miles west of Route 495 in Boylston, high atop a hill overlooking the

Wachusett reservoir. We started going there about ten years ago, and have seen it become ever more beautiful with every passing year. The website is www.towerhillbg.org. We like to visit there in every season, but there is nothing quite like the spring. This month visitors to the Seven States Daffodil Show can expect a special treat, even if I am blowing my own trumpet.

# CYCLES OF LIFE
## May 2005

Four years have passed since I last saw my brother Sean in 2001. Now, after a visit of but four days, I watch as he straps on his bicycle helmet and prepares to leave for work. We hug a last goodbye and I turn to walk towards the bus that will take my mother and me to the car rental office. We are leaving the city of Coventry and heading back to Bournemouth on the south coast of England, where my younger brother Nigel lives.

Our route takes us through Oxford, the town where my mother, my brothers and I all were born. The motorways and bypasses, which nowadays offer speedy transit from place to place, beckon us to hasten our journey, but it is the old ways which call out to me, as they do each time I come home. The country roads with steep embankments and curving hedgerows over which our family of five would ride, three boys squeezed into the back seat, with Nigel, being the smallest, forced into the middle.

Coming into Oxford I see the signpost for Horton-cum-Studley and cannot resist. We grew up in Headington Quarry near the London Road out of Oxford. In 1962 when I was about ten and Sean eleven we had recently acquired our first bikes.  His was a blue Palm Beach, mine a red with white mudguards.  One early summer's day we decided to take a long and daring bike ride, all the way to Horton and back again.  Sean persuaded me that I could do it.  Now as Mum and I retrace the route in our rented car, we pass the familiar places of my childhood.  Driving down the hill of Bayswater Road, I see the house where our babysitter, an older teenager named Jean, used to live, and I remember how, as we got a little older,  we could sit in our front room at night and persuade her to let us stay up past our bedtime, promising not to tell.

The drive to Horton is surprisingly short.  After a mere five miles we are sweeping down to the bottom of the hill and into the village.  I recognize the pub on the corner, where Sean and I sat outside and rested before taking the long journey home.  It had been an easy ride up to that point, and as we celebrated having reached our outbound destination, I did not realize that the easy downhill journey would be transformed into a hard climb home.

Driving back now I see how long and steep the uphill must have seemed to me then, and as we come almost to the crest of the hill, I stop the car beneath a glade of trees.  I see the gate into the open field and remember the frustration and fear that beset me as a little boy standing  beside my bike amidst the cow parsley blossoming head high on the embankment.   I cried and wondered how I would ever get home.

Sean came back and walked me to the top of the hill, waited while I recovered my strength, and we eventually set off and returned home safely. Today, I pull out my camera and photograph the spot.

Driving back into Headington we pass the crematorium where only four short years after that day in 1962 my grandfather was interred. As always on these journeys, we return to Quarry High Street and the house where I was born. Small alleyways lead off the street and my mother and I walk along them. "This is where Dad and I did a lot of our courting," she tells me in one spot. In another I remember my first hesitant attempts to stay astride a bicycle as Dad alternately held me and released me, trying to teach me how to keep my balance. I remember the triumph of finally moving on my own two wheels down the alley.

After a short stop in Headington, we go on to Sandford where my grandparents lived. Sean and I would bicycle there on a Saturday morning and spend the morning fishing in the Thames, catching nothing but each other's lines, and, on one occasion, a swan who happily escaped.

Leaving Oxford, I once again choose the old route which we used to take when we went on holidays to Bournemouth, before we all moved there in 1964. Travelling across the green crests of the downs, through bucolic villages like Sutton Courtenay and Clifton Hampden, I realize that I will never take the bike ride I once thought Sean and I might take, retracing my father's route in 1946 when he and a friend attempted to ride the 90 miles from Oxford to Bournemouth.

Now Dad has been gone for 22 years. Sean tucks white hair into his helmet as he cycles to work in the mornings. In five days I will be saying goodbye to Nigel and Mum and boarding a plane for Boston. I have lived in Concord for thirty years wondering how these memories can remain so crystal clear and yet seem so remote as if from the dream of another life. Three small boys, who once sat shoulder to shoulder in the back of a Morris Minor, now live their lives spread over three thousand miles, and bonds that were formed over fifty years ago still tie our hearts together.

# VACATION MEMORIES
## July 2005

Diane and I just came back from Vermont after a short stay in the Northeast Kingdom. We first discovered this beautiful part of New England nineteen years ago, when Diane saw an advertisement for The Wildflower Inn in Lyndonville. It seemed like, and turned out to be, the perfect place to stay when the colors turn brilliant in the fall. We have returned there several times over the years, mostly in September or October, but twice in the winter as well. We had never visited in the summer before this year.

When we first visited in 1986, the inn-keepers, Jim and Mary O'Reilly, had just opened the inn in an old farmhouse atop the aptly named Darling Hill, and were the young parents of four children, the youngest just a baby. Nineteen years later the baby is working as the assistant inn-keeper and has four additional younger siblings all now helping out at the inn. The inn itself has been developed over the years, with new suites and renovated cottages looking north-westward over rolling hills towards Mount Pisgah and Lake Willoughby. On the eastward side of the ridge stands Burke Mountain, a seemingly timeless backdrop watching over this shifting human activity. In front of the old farmhouse bountiful perennial gardens bloom with blue irises and white peonies, which will give way to purple asters and maroon 'Autumn Joy' sedum in September.

Vacations have often seemed to me like little lives. Plucked from the protective womb of my daily cares and routines, for the first few days I move from initial disorientation into a sense of presence, enjoying new experiences, looking at everything with new eyes, taking each moment sometimes with pleasure, sometimes with trepidation. With no quotidian structure to move me mindlessly through my life, there is time to bask in the sunlight, reflect and wonder in the shadows.

The nineteen years since we first visited this little haven seem more like five, but we were in our thirties then, and will be well into our seventies if we keep returning for a further nineteen. When we first went there, we took a pair of bicycles and tried to discover as much of the picturesque surrounding countryside as possible. We found that we were never as happy as when we simply stayed atop the hill and walked along the ridge taking in the breathtaking, panoramic views at our doorstep. This year we parked the car on day one and ignored it until it was time to leave.

Walking each day along the hilltop, we found ourselves and each other removed from the minute-to-minute demands of home and work and garden. Carrying a camera, I tried as always to capture images of the surrounding nature, vainly attempting to hold fast to fleeting moments of mid-summer. Sitting together out amongst the summer wildflowers under a vast and cloudless sky, it sometimes seemed as if time might stand still or one could wish it to do so, as if we might hold fast to each other and this moment forever. As the warm breezes scattered the pollens over the hillside, joys and sorrows, love and hope and loss, past and future seemed to coalesce in the now.

I still remember the very first time that time stood still for me this way. I was eleven years old and on vacation in Bournemouth in England. My two brothers, one older, one younger, had been at loggerheads for the entire two weeks, agreeing only on the proposition that they did not like each other, a condition my young self mistakenly imagined to be tragic and irreversible. It was the last day of our vacation. I had just finished primary school and was about to enter the next tier of my education in September at a new school in our hometown of Oxford. About to be a little fish in a big pond, as our headmistress cautioned us. Everything was changing.

We used to stay in a block of flats called Parade Court on the cliff-top overlooking Bournemouth beach. It was a foggy morning ("heat haze" Dad used to call it) and I had walked down to the beach alone after breakfast. Wrapped in the cool sea mist I was kneeling on the damp sand where yesterday's sandcastles had been washed away by the overnight tide. The beach was deserted. Seagulls hovered over the erosion-scarred cliffs. As I watched the waves rising and falling, approaching and receding, I felt a profound sadness to see this family vacation slip away, feeling without yet fully understanding the transitory nature of life.

On our last evening in Vermont, Diane and I came out from our dinner at The Wildflower Inn to be greeted by the perfect semicircle of a rainbow arcing sublimely over Burke Mountain. As usual, my first instinct was to reach for the camera, but having put the image onto film, we stood a while and simply gazed until the colors gradually melted into the twilight. It was the most ephemeral of sights, an object of no substance now recorded weakly on a glossy piece of paper inside a photo album, but as we watched hand in hand while it faded from the sky, I felt the moment imprinting itself firmly amidst the store of my memories.

# PLAIN SAILING
## August 2005

I have often thought that life seems liking sailing a boat. Navigating through the vagaries of chance and fate, one's own intention finds its way to shore by some mysterious interaction of forces. Never in control, as we go through life we somehow get better at reading the currents, knowing when to "go with the flow", charting a course.

I first came to this country thirty years ago. I was twenty-three years old and scarcely at the helm of my own life. Having graduated from college in 1974, I was at a loss as to how to make the great leap from being a schoolboy and student to starting a career. It has sometimes seemed to me, that one almost forgotten moment in 1972 changed my life forever without my even knowing it. I had been studying in Germany, and had arranged to go home to England for Christmas. I had answered an advertisement to share a ride in a VW beetle from Freiburg in the south of Germany to London, a little more than a twenty-four hour trip, I recall.

The driver of the car accepted me as a passenger along with five others. So we crowded very uncomfortably into the tiny car. In such confined quarters, I found it hard to communicate with anyone in the car other than the person next to me, who more or less obliterated my view of the others. In the front passenger seat there was a young student from Atlanta, Georgia, traveling to England for the first time to visit his girlfriend. When we were all finally pried loose from the car in London, he and I were dropped at Waterloo station so that we could take trains to the South. We had not spoken together until then, but he asked me how to use the public phone. I waited while he tried unsuccessfully to reach his girlfriend.

It was an unprecedentedly magnanimous gesture for me, but when I saw that he was at a loss, alone in a foreign country, I invited him to take the train with me, come and spend the night with the friends I was visiting, and then travel the short distance to his destination the following day. Thus began a short-lived and somewhat casual friendship, which we picked up when we returned to Freiburg in January. More significantly he was the first and it seems essential link in the chain of people I met, whereby I decided to come to the United States for a short visit in 1975. I had no idea what I was going to do with the rest of my life, but I found it here.

Concord was the first place I came to after arriving on a flight into JFK on a sultry August evening. New York was a city that fulfilled every expectation of a young Englishman whose vision of this country was almost entirely determined by television. After traveling through the night on a bus to Natick, I was met by friends who drove me to Concord. I still recall vividly the morning sun illuminating the loosestrife around Fairhaven Bay as I caught my first true glimpses of the town I have lived in ever since.

Thirty years later, I have carved out my niche with a career in natural foods right here in this town, spending twenty-five years as manager at Concord Spice & Grain, and now the last five and a half at Debra's Natural Gourmet.

When my parents first came to visit in 1978, I remember my father telling me that he had emigrated from Ireland to England during the Second World War to help in the war effort. Ireland was a neutral country, so he obtained his release from the Irish National Army to come across the water as a war worker. He hoped that once in England he might enlist in the American forces. After performing his service he hoped he might then be demobilized in the States, resume his career as an entertainer, and perhaps achieve a dream of getting to Broadway. By entering England as a war worker, however, he found that he was contractually obligated to remain such. When he met my mother after the war, his life found its new direction.

When I was twelve years old, my family moved to Bournemouth, my parents bought a corner shop and started a little grocery store which they named R.J. Leahy & Sons. Dad thought it would be "a little gold-mine." It turned out disastrously, corner shops being a dying breed in 1964. They lost all their investment, and we just managed to exit without bankruptcy. For the first months we were there though, my brothers and I always wanted to help out in the store.

My first real job in the summers of 1969 and 1970 was working with my mother at a bakery counter in a department store in the town. I also worked there on Saturdays during the school-year. When my mother was on vacation in the second summer, the company brought in a semi-retired relief manager for the two weeks. She had only been used to running small corner shop bakeries. With my mother's counsel from home, I quietly helped her.

When I graduated from college in 1974, I had no real idea of what was next. With a degree in German and History, I thought perhaps my best option would be teaching. Since I had most enjoyed literature, I also had the fantasy that perhaps one day I could write. But all my work experience was in retail, and somehow that was the only employment that seemed real to me.

Thirty years later I wonder at how I found a life that seems to suit me so well. I enjoy working at something that has real meaning to me. Bringing good foods to the community, supporting organic farmers, promoting healthy lifestyles all align with values that are important to me. Working with people I like in a truly communal spirit is very rewarding. Over the years I also spent some time teaching German at

Concord Carlisle Adult Education, and today, contributing to *The Concord Journal,* I even enjoy making my mark as a writer.

Embarking on this journey as a confused youth with no real plan for my life, somehow I found the haven of a wife I love, work I embrace, friendships I enjoy. A chance meeting with a stranger, a magnanimous gesture, unknowingly fulfilling a part of my father's dream, blending my early work experience with my own expectations, somehow all these elements of choice and chance and fate have formed the tapestry of a life.

# THE PRIZE

## September 2005

As children return to school with a mixture of hope, trepidation, resignation and resentment, my mind drifts back to Oxford in 1963. I was eleven when I saw my first Prize Day. I had been at Salesian College for boys for about two weeks when it came around. All the boys in uniform and all the parents in their best suits gathered in the town center and filed into the grand hallway of the Oxford University building, where the event was being held. I sat up on the balcony with all the other first-year boys and our parents. The older boys sat down in the main auditorium, from which they could easily walk up to the stage to receive the prizes that they were being awarded for their previous year's achievements. I watched with envy as one boy after another went up to the podium, shook hands with Father Archer, the headmaster, and proudly accepted the mysterious small parcel which had lain on the table awaiting him. I knew I could be eligible to be down there next year.

Dad had often told us about the prize he had won in 1933. It was a special prize created just for Dad. "Nobby Barry was the dean," he used to tell us, as he combed our hair. "He was a dapper little chap." He would often tell the other boys to follow the example of Dad's appearance. Dad was proud of his well-shone shoes, his jet-black hair, his manicured hands, but on Prize Day it was a complete surprise when they announced the new prize. "The Dean's Prize for Deportment to Richard Leahy."

I studied hard in my first year at the new school, and at the end of each term I finished second in my class. I knew that prizes were given to the top three boys. I looked forward to Prize Day all summer. That was the summer that we moved to Bournemouth. My parents bought a little corner shop, and we were trying to start a new life there.

In September 1964 I started at my new school, but I was determined to go back to Oxford for Prize Day. Dad had taken me to see Father Archer so that we could find out when it was to take place, and I could come back and receive my reward. He wasn't there, but one of the other priests told us they had not decided on a date yet. When we didn't hear anything I wrote to the headmaster to remind him. I really wanted to attend the ceremony, but if I could not be there, I at least wanted my prize sent to me. I didn't hear from him.

It was Christmas when we went back to Oxford for the first time. Things weren't going well at the shop, but Mum and Dad didn't want to tell Gran and Granddad how bad it was, so we pretended we were happy there. I didn't like the new school as much. I hadn't really made any friends, and I had finished seventeenth at the end of my first term there. On Boxing Day I went over to see my friend Garvin. At first

I was too embarrassed to ask him, but eventually I found a way to pose the question. "Whatever happened about Prize Day?"

He looked a little sheepish at first and then pulled down a thin hard-bound book from the bookcase, an abridged version of *Moby Dick*. At first I thought perhaps he was going to present it to me, that he had been holding it for me. I opened it up and read his name printed on the inside of the cover. He had finished fifth in class, but since two boys ahead of him had left, they forfeited their prizes, and he moved up to third. I hid my disappointment.

A few weeks later on a cold night in January, we were in the living room at the back of the shop when Dad told me he had something for me. I had just finished my homework. "This came for you today." He handed me a thick brown envelope with my name and address written on it but no stamp. I opened it curiously, not really noticing the smile on his face. I pulled out a heavy hardbound book with a red dust-jacket: *The Oxford Shakespeare: Complete Works*. I turned to the first page and read the inscription.

"To James Leahy to mark his splendid achievements in the first year at Salesian College, Cowley, Oxford, 1963-1964."

"How did this come?" I asked doubtfully. Dad smiled. He said they couldn't deny me it now. I had earned the prize. I looked at the inscription again. And then I realized. "But this is your handwriting, Dad!"

He tried to think of something to say, but I didn't need him to pretend. I missed having my fleeting moment of pride on Prize Day, and I was still upset that the school would just forget about me, but forty years later *The Oxford Shakespeare* has a special place on the bookshelf in my study. Today, as I turn to Sonnet 29, I read the words of the bard:

"...............love remember'd such wealth brings
that then I scorn to change my state with kings."

# LETTING GO
## November 2005

On Veterans Day twenty-three years ago my father died. I had been playing tennis on the morning of November 9th, when my brother Nigel called to say Dad had had a stroke and might not even last the day. Diane came down to the tennis court to tell me. I was on the next plane to England. Nigel met me at the airport and we rushed to the hospital.

It's hard to say I got there in time. In time for what? In time for him to still open his eyes for one last time and try to speak when I came to his bed? In time to tell him I loved him? In time to sit with him for the last twenty-four hours of his life, wondering if the morphine washed away all consciousness of his parting?

I had seen him only a few weeks earlier, when I had visited England to attend my brother Sean's wedding. He had been bed-ridden most of the summer with a post-operative infection, and had seemed older, shorter of breath. Nigel said he thought it had taken a lot out of him. Saying our sad good-bye at Heathrow airport, my imagination telescoped forward, realizing that if we saw each other only once a year, I might have only a countable number of visits with him left. Our future foreshortened through this lens. I wanted to extend that view to infinity, or at least beyond my vision. I did not realize that I had reached the end of the count.

I had been working in the natural food industry for seven years, and my reformer's zeal gnawed at me to convert my family, to keep everyone alive and healthy. I wasn't ready to see my Dad get old, to say goodbye completely. But who was I to change his habits, interfere with his likes? What book would I have given him, I had wondered. I had considered sending him a copy of *Are You Confused?* by Paavo Airola. Paavo Airola was one of the leading nutritionists of the time and his books were popular and accessible. Maybe I could have interested Dad.

Now as I watched him die, I wondered, if I could have changed all this. Maybe Mum wouldn't be laying on the hospital bed with him, knowing this would be the last time their heads would meet together on a pillow. And Sean and Nigel and I would not be there, waiting for the gurgling in his lungs to cease.

"You can't change another person," Nigel reassured me afterwards. "He wouldn't have been Dad then. He lived his life the way he wanted to. It was his life. It doesn't matter how long it was when all is said and done."

I knew he was right. Love is not measured in years. A century from now would anyone say his was less of a life, because it lasted sixty-six years instead of seventy-six or eighty-six? All I could do was love him, let him live his life, give to him freely, without condition; just love him as he had loved me. Just love him.

He did last for twenty-four hours after I arrived. We only left his room when the nurses needed to turn him over. The nurses let my mother spend the night in his room on a cot, and they gave me a cot up the stairs in a closet. Sean and Nigel went home and slept with the phone by their beds.

"Wake us the minute there's any change," we all insisted. At four o'clock in the morning the night nurse thought he was going to die, and we all rushed back down to him, but he gasped fitfully through.

It was after that, that Mum climbed up onto the bed with him, and lay with her arm around him. When the doctor came to look at him, we all went into the common room for a while and then I went back in to sit with him by myself for a few moments. I wanted a few moments alone with him. I put my hand on his tired head, stroked my fingers across the thin strands of white hair.

I whispered to him as I ran my fingers across his head, trying to conjure images of flowing and releasing, wondering what miracles an apostate son could channel. I tried to bathe him in soft words. I wanted to bring him back to us, but I couldn't even maintain my own hope. I knew I was saying goodbye.

"It's time to turn him over" the nurse said. She had entered the room quietly. "You can come back in a minute." I kissed his head and placed it gently back on the pillow,

"It didn't work" I thought to myself as I left the room. "Nothing happened." I sat in the common room with Mum and Nigel and Sean. I was there for barely two minutes when another nurse came running down the hall.

"You'd better come quickly!" she said.

"Has he died?" None of us asked.

We rushed into the room. They had propped him up on the pillows, but we could see immediately the stillness. The vein that had been bulging on his left temple was flat and empty. He was gray-complexioned and soundless. Lifeless.

I think we must have all touched him simultaneously. Nigel and I had his left hand, Mum and Sean his right. He started, heaved one final parting breath, as if he had saved it for us and fell back for the last time.

When we took Mum home later in the morning, she combed her hair in the bedroom mirror. I remember feeling relieved that she still wanted to take care of herself now. I wondered about all her lonely tomorrows. I wondered about that book again. Could I have changed this?

When I came back to the U.S. after the funeral, I still felt that I had failed in that last moment in the hospital room, but somewhere along the way I have come to realize that I had only failed my own expectations, my own wish to hang on to him. Perhaps I had given him something. Perhaps I had even helped to release him, caressing his head as he let go of life.

Dad was sixty-six years old when he died.

A week after I came home I read in the paper that Paavo Airola had had a stroke and died. At the age of sixty-six.

"Just love him!" I thought to myself.

# FOR AULD LANG SYNE
## January 2006

I was twelve years old the first time I remember hearing *Auld Lang Syne*. I wanted to cry. It was 1964 and my older brother Sean and I were staying with my grandparents in Oxford in England. Our family had moved to Bournemouth on the south coast only three months before, but we had come back to visit for Christmas. My parents and my younger brother Nigel returned to Bournemouth after Boxing Day, but Sean and I remained for the week at my grandparents' club. Our stay culminated with the New Year's Eve Dance in the barn, and we were allowed to stay up until midnight to see the New Year in.

As the countdown to 1965 began, my grandparents, aunts and uncles, family friends, club members all linked hands and began to sing. At first the words were confusing to me. Not recognizing the subjunctive form or the poetic word order, I was confused by the lyrics. "May old acquaintance be forgot" seemed to be more a recommendation than a lament, but the plaintive tone, and the strangely evocative words "auld lang syne" conveyed the sentiment fully.

Up until that summer I had lived in an unchanging world. The old were old, the young were young, and everyone seemed to be fixed in their place. Whenever my dad met a friend from long ago, the first thing he said was, "You haven't changed a bit." My great grandmother had died a few years before, but I had only ever known her as a frail old person, and even though we children were growing up, it seemed to be only slowly. We didn't seem to be gaining on anybody.

Now as the revelers at the barn dance repeated the chorus, I felt tears welling up more and more, and it seemed as if time was shifting very slowly beneath me like beach sand tugging at the soles of my feet with the receding tide.

Forty-one years later the undertow becomes ever stronger and faster. 1964 was the first year I recall being aware of the Olympic Games, which had taken place in Tokyo. It would feel like almost another decade before they were staged the next time in Mexico. Today they seem like an almost annual event. When I was a boy 1984 was a faraway future described by George Orwell. Today I can hardly believe that it is a twenty year old memory from a past millennium.

My very first memory turned fifty years old two months ago on Nigel's fiftieth birthday. To be honest, I am no longer sure if it is a memory or a picture I have painted, because I was constantly reminded as a child of the cuteness of my words. Standing in front of the tiny cot in my parents' bedroom I saw my younger brother for the first time and asked, "Can it talk?" Memory or image, I can clearly see the corner of the room, the cot by the wardrobe, the sleeping baby, and I can feel Sean standing beside me as my mother sits up in bed behind us, and my father proudly shows us the new arrival.

It was the first of a lifetime of memories gathered as each year turns to the next, and I have walked through life amongst people I have loved. This year marked the thirtieth anniversary of my coming to this country. It is twenty-one years since my wife Diane and I bought our first house, where we still live today sowing new memories daily.

As a boy, I often found it tiresome that older people loved to reminisce so much. My father could talk for hours about his younger days in Ireland, the country he had left forever when he married my mother. Now I find myself doing the very same thing, as with every passing year the preciousness of memory seems greater, and it seems to me that the strange paradox of memory is that it is simultaneously both all that we have and all that we have lost. Our joy and our sorrow. Both grief and consolation.

Much as I believe in living in the present, it is the past that is the great treasure trove of experience, the harvest of a lifetime, and I sometimes think that one of my greatest sorrows about dying is that I would no longer be here to have all those memories.

I have long enjoyed photography, often using it as an attempt to hold onto all these moments of the past. Yet some of the most vivid pictures exist most firmly or even solely in my memory. The ferry ride from Martha's Vineyard when Diane and I returned from our honeymoon. Standing together in a town-square in Provo, Utah under the vast western sky at sunset on our only trip to the West in 1993. Sitting on a beach together in Rockport at twilight watching the tide go out. Finding a rainbow over the mountains of northern Vermont as the last light of day faded from the evening sky.

Now as 2005 turns to 2006 and we look to the future, we will hope to keep filling our granaries for a few more years, and when I call my gray-haired baby brother in England I will remember how often I have rejoiced that it can talk.

# EQUINOX
## March 2006

I first saw our snowdrops blooming over a month ago. Our warm weeks in February seemed to be promising an early spring. Amidst the brown and shriveled blades of grass the small white blossoms endured the subsequent snows and freezes as steadfast harbingers of the season to come. Now the equinox has finally arrived. Light of day has equaled dark of night and is on the ascendant.

Last week Diane and I went in to see the New England Spring Flower Show in Boston. On a sunny sixty-degree day, winter seemed to be losing its grip. Inside the Bayside Exposition Center we were greeted by green lawns, beds of colorful annuals, blooming azaleas, lupins and delphiniums, a white moonlit garden with sequin stars. This year's theme was "Welcome Home." As I do each year, I closed my eyes and ran my fingers across the warm soft grass to touch as well as see and smell the spring.

At home the first of our pots of forced daffodils has started to produce blooms. White perianths surround cups which opened yellow and grow richer in color with every passing day, achieving their full orange glow as each flower matures. Its name is 'Chromacolor.' Companion pots of other varieties are lined up alongside it awaiting their turn. In the garden beds the first green tips are breaking through the brown of last year's decaying leaves.

Last Sunday we ventured out into the backyard and raked away the twigs and sometimes boughs of linden and pine which our recent winds had strewn across the lawn. We flattened the small uplifts of earth where animals had dug in search of grubs last November. We evened out the ground where vole tracks meandered through yellow desiccated grass. Gradually our small environment transformed itself from a winter wasteland into something tidy and hopeful. I remembered an evening last summer when I had stood outside after mowing the full green lawn and surveyed our beds of daylilies, rudbeckia, echinacea, nepeta and the first blushes of sedum 'Autumn Joy'. The hours of raking, spreading compost, digging, dividing, spreading organic fertilizer, all seemed to repay me in that moment. Now the first blisters of spring returned that promise. The winter of our discontent to be made glorious summer.

And yet as nature reawakens hope all around us, it seems that it is civilization that is red in tooth and claw. How do we rejoice in the beauty of our tiny gardens, when our global village seems to be in a state of civil war?

When I was in college studying history, I came to believe that there was some sense of continual progress in the human condition. That education and prosperity would eventually become the accepted birthright of all people. That some kind of real and true democracy was inexorably on the march. Today I so often feel a sense of hopelessness, as I see both my native and my adopted countries and most of our civilized western world alternately sponsoring tyrants then righteously going to war with them, bringing untold suffering to millions. The torment of intractable conflicts across the globe destroys all parties to it, and our children, like Shakespeare's Romeo and Juliet, become "poor sacrifices of our enmity." With so much to fear in this world, I find I am often more frightened by what "we" might do next than what "they" will do next.

So even as we pass our vernal equinox, one can feel that darkness threatens to overpower light completely, and hope can seem as scant as a snowdrop in February. How do we preserve our humanity in a world that has grown ever smaller even as our destructive capabilities have become immense? We can never banish darkness, nor persuade it to become light, but we must somehow shine as much light into the darkness in whatever ways we know.

I have no idea how to create a better world; I make a better pacifist than an activist, but somehow I hope that attempting to act from conscience and compassion even in the tiniest ways can be added to the sum of the light of the world. Ray Mong growing organically at Applefield Farm, Tom Sisson producing homegrown eggs and honey, Mary Jane Wuensch commuting to work on a bicycle, the volunteers at Open Table feeding those in need, the late Carola Domar offering support to caregivers in Concord can be added to the work of Alan Lightman building schools in Cambodia, and Paul Farmer and Partners in Health fighting infectious disease in Haiti, so that our world will not be entirely surrendered to darkness.

# TEACHERS
## June 2006

In the middle of April a fourth-grade teacher from the Thoreau School, Susan Erickson, came into Debra's Natural Gourmet and asked if one of us might be interested in talking to a small group of students about organic foods. The class was about to make their end-of-year movie and wanted to arrange interviews with various people. It seemed like a worthwhile and fun project, so I volunteered with only the mildest trepidation. They set up a time in early May.

About a week before the interview the class provided me with a list of their questions. I was somewhat baffled at first when I found that all of the questions related to the presence of acids in foods, whether or not organic foods contained acids, and whether the acids in organic foods were preferable. I soon found out that the class had been studying acids, looking into the pH of various foods, and had come up with a number of questions concerning acids and the environment.

In early May the three students, Isabelle Williams, Sophie Holin, and Tessa Hanselman from the Thoreau School arrived at the store along with the instructional technology specialist, Sue Howard. Looking at the earnest and intelligent faces of three nine-year-olds who had been studying acids for the past several weeks, I realized that they probably knew more than I did about some of these questions. They told me what they had been learning, and we talked about additives in food, what we mean by 'natural' and 'organic', what to look for when reading labels. I was impressed by their questions, their responses and their attentive approach. It was a great pleasure to work with them. Their willing interest and curiosity seemed to evoke the best in me.

In the first week of June, Susan Erickson returned to the store with an invitation to come and watch the film, which was to be shown to students and parents at the Thoreau School at the end of the school year. By a happy circumstance the movie was being shown during the week of my vacation, when my mother would be visiting from England. This student and his parent accepted the invitation.

We arrived on the Friday a little after noon. We were a few minutes late as we had gone first to the wrong Thoreau School. I expected to slip quietly into the back of the auditorium, but instead I was treated as a guest of honour at a premiere, and my mother and I were formally escorted by Isabelle, from the film crew, to a seat in the front row. It was no surprise that the students had done a great job with their film, nor was I surprised to find that they had indeed learned more than I knew on the subject of acids. My only surprise was when, on watching myself being interviewed at the Natural Gourmet, I did not immediately recognize myself addressing the three children. "It's Granddad," I thought. I thanked him silently for what he had taught me.

When the film was over we were all invited to lunch, after which one more surprise was unveiled. Mrs. Erickson had made a film to commemorate this fourth grade class. She spoke about what a special group of kids they were, how great they were to teach, and how much she had learned from them. Her film, a movingly affectionate collage of portraits and groups taken during many moments of the year, was backed by a medley of musical pieces including 'Getting to Know You' and 'The Old Schoolyard'. The rolling of the credits was a thank-you to the students for making her a better teacher. I remembered Sister Lisetta.

When I was nine years old, I entered my last two years of primary school, in which I was to be taught by Sister Lisetta. As a smaller boy, I had always been a little afraid of her. She taught the older boys and had the appearance of possessing the quality most apt to strike fear in an eight-year-old boy. She looked strict. How wrong I was.

Forty-five years later I remember her still. I remember her not for what she taught, although I do still recall reciting the speech of the Great Spirit from Hiawatha under her tutelage. I remember her because she instilled confidence and belief in myself; because she cared. I'm sure most if not all of the class shared in this experience. She sent us forth two years later a little more ready to embark on the next phase of our education. For several years I felt the gentle hand of her guidance, the encouragement of her expectations.

An afternoon at the Thoreau School reminded me of the difference that a nurturing teacher can make to the children in his or her care. When I left primary school in 1963, I had learned to read and to write, to add and to subtract. I knew the counties of England and the countries of the world, but the greatest gifts are those that are given in love: from parents, grandparents, uncles and aunts, and siblings, and from teachers who care.

# THOSE DYING GENERATIONS
## September 2006

A short while ago, while looking through the DVD section of the Maynard Public Library, I came across an old favorite *Masterpiece Theater* series from the 1980's. Adapted from the novel by R. E. Delderfield, *To Serve Them All My Days* tells the story of a young man returning shell-shocked from the trenches of World War I. The series follows its hero, David Powlett-Jones, as he takes up and pursues a career as a schoolteacher at a private school, which Delderfield calls Bamfylde. The location for Bamfylde was the school of Milton Abbey near the Dorset coast, where my family came to live when I was twelve.

Watching it again, after twenty-some years, nourished my nostalgic soul. The series itself covers a period of a little more than twenty years, mostly from the 1920's into the 1940's, the world of my parents and grandparents. Although I was not born until 1952, I often feel that I am as much a child of the early part of the twentieth century.

My egg came into the world in 1925 when my mother was born in Marston just outside Oxford. I grew up in Oxford during the years following World War II in the imagined world of a child, a world received from parents and grandparents, made simpler by the innocence of childhood, and described by the simple verities passed on to me by those who had gone before.

I have always found that any novel or television series that spans twenty or more years, covering births and deaths, encompassing careers and lifetimes, seems to foreshorten time for the viewer. What has begun soon comes to an ending. Observed lives can be seen in whole. The older I become, the more I realize that I can look at my own story through this same telescope.

Watching the series, I found myself caught up in the sweep of the characters' lives, their changes, the changing world between the world wars, the passing of a way of life, the young becoming older, W.B. Yeats' "dying generations".

Layered over that were my own memories. Drifting back through time I remembered that twenty years ago at the beginning of the 1980's when the program was produced, I was still a young man, only recently arrived in this country. My wife Diane and I were just beginning our life together. The future ahead still seemed almost without end. I was yet unaware that my father would die in 1982.

Twenty years earlier, in the 1960's, I was a boy at a private school in Bournemouth. I remember playing rugby at Milton Abbey when I was fourteen and fifteen. Rising up from its bucolic setting near the Dorset coast, the abbey was an impressive host to boys who came to muddy their knees upon the rugby field and then be taken in for afternoon tea and scones in the great hall. At fifteen years of age I recall we were torn between amusement and horror that the boys of Milton Abbey were still required to wear a school uniform that featured short trousers. As the sixties seemed to be pulling us out of some of our innocence, tradition strove to tug us back. The stable world of childhood was giving way to oncoming adulthood. I suffered my first loss when my granddad died in 1966.

Another twenty years before that, during the forties, the period to which *To Serve Them All My Days* took its narrative, my father came to England from Ireland. Working in the factories in Oxord to help the war effort, he endured the blacked-out nights listening for German aircraft. On the other side of Oxford my mother was a schoolgirl forced to sleep many nights in the bomb shelter while her father, my granddad, walked the streets as an air-raid warden. After the war my parents met and married, and in 1952 they hatched that twenty-seven year old egg that was me.

Two decades further back, Granddad had come home from the Royal Marines after World War I. He and Gran met in the 1920's. He was twenty-five and she was twenty-three when my mother was born in 1925. Gran lived to be 93. The last time I saw her was at my mother's seventieth birthday party. She lived through all but a handful of years of the twentieth century.

Grand-dad was born in 1899. As a child, I thought that the nineteenth century seemed like the other end of history. Looking back in these twenty-year increments a century seems closer to how a decade used to feel. With every passing year the pace of time shifts ever more from glacial to rapid transit, leaving us "sick with desire and fastened to a dying animal" in the words of Yeats.

Sitting in front of the flickering television screen today, the private school world of the 1920's seems like my own world. It was the world which was being shaped for me to receive in 1952, the traces of which I felt throughout childhood, the memories of which I carry still.

# AFTER THANKSGIVING
## November 2006

There is something very restful about this time of year. As the darkness falls around us and we brace ourselves for winter's bite, there is yet the relief of another season's work completed.

Yesterday Diane and I completed the last big task of autumn. A warm 60-degree day was perfect for trimming the 38 arbor vitae and one yew that ring our property. Last week I spent a gray Saturday raking and shredding the millions (or was it billions?) of leaves that two days of rain and wind had spread across the half acre we call home. Ground-up gray and papery linden leaves, maroon and leathery pear tree leaves, crispy brown oak and yellow maple leaves all now form a multi-colored mulch banked round the bases of shrubs and layered in garden beds protecting perennials. The lawn mower limping with its loose drive belt made one last trip across the lawn. Its horsepower provided the cutting; my manpower much of the pushing. I shall have it serviced for next spring.

So now as I look around me, there is the satisfaction of a well-tended yard. Dried hydrangea blossoms dance outside the kitchen window. Last week a single rudbeckia blossom was still hanging on like the reflection of one last drop of golden summer sun. The intervening frosts have since shriveled it.

By February I am sure I will be eagerly anticipating another spring, but right now I am savoring the rest. The gardening season began with crocuses in March and has kept us busy ever since. Dandelion digging began in April. By May we had picked up all the twigs of winter's pruning, uncovered and divided plants in our perennial beds, spread two yards of compost and three yards of bark mulch, circumambulated the lawn once with organic fertilizer and multiple times with the lawn mower, pruned the quince for the first time. Azaleas, hollies, lilacs took their turn facing secateurs and shears. Suckers were removed from the base of the linden trees, and hanging boughs were lopped or sawn and dragged over to the brush pile. The weigela was pruned and staked where snowfall from the roof had opened it.

More organic lawn fertilizer in June. With plenty of summer rain the grass grew lush and long each week keeping the mower busy. In July and August we plucked spent daylilies every morning, turning our fingers red and gold and purple with their juices. By hand we removed excess crabgrass and plantain in the summer's heat.

September brought one last lawn fertilization, and by the end of the month pine needles swept across the lawn and fat red berries lay around the dogwood tree. In October Diane cut down dried stalks of heliopsis, rudbeckia, hemerocallis, eupatorium, peony, and we planted 330 daffodil and tulip bulbs. The leaves seemed to turn early this year, but yet it still took most of the month of November to finally bring them down.

And finally the arbor vitae. I always wait until after the first frost to prune, having learned that I might otherwise disturb a hive of bees or a nest of hornets. Sometimes the opportunity seems to be escaping as the demands of fall cleanup and the vagaries of the weather variously determine. One year I spent a seventy-degree New Year's Day pruning after I had thought I might have missed my chance.

So now we sit back and take a breath. Amidst the smoky autumnal skies, dusk just after midday, the gray filigree of bare trees, the brown hydrangea pom-poms and frilly heads of dried Autumn Joy, a handful of shiny red berries on the viburnum as yet uneaten by the birds, there is a stillness.

Below the ground, plants are rooting and gathering up for the winter. Spring bulbs which were dormant all summer are returning to life. Grape hyacinth have already sent up their shaggy green foliage in preparation for another year. Alongside the front of the house, where last week's torrential rains washed away a small channel of soil, tips of daffodils pushing up for next spring have been exposed. The thrice-pruned quince, perhaps our most vigorous shrub, is showing tiny red buds that will produce next year's scarlet blossoms. Even as I release the burden of the year's work, I cannot help but look ahead. I spread a couple of inches of topsoil over the exposed daffodils to tuck them in for the winter.

Stopped between satisfaction and hope, between relief and anticipation, I return indoors to the warmth of home. It is a time to read, to write, to rest a little, and maybe we can have a few weeks before I have to go out to shovel snow.

# HYACINTHS & HOLLYHOCKS
## March 2007

Spring is here once again. The objective measures confirm the fact. The Ides of March has passed, the equinox is behind us. The length of the days, the angle of the afternoon sun, bulbs breaking through the ground, all welcome us to the new season. The lion and the lamb are changing places not without the occasional roar amidst the bleating.

For a while this year we may have wondered if we would have a winter. On January 6, Diane and I spent a seventy-degree day in T-shirts raking fallen twigs. We wondered if we would ever see snow this winter, but the cold arrived at last, and snow, of course, waited almost until spring. I am not one who is susceptible to the puritanical notion that pleasure is undeserved unless earned by pain, and I do not particularly like the cold any more than I enjoy shoveling snow. Nevertheless, there was something disquieting about the seeming absence of winter a few months ago. I look forward eagerly to spring each year, but to have it thrust upon us too early was unsettling.

It is not just that winter is a time of rest for gardeners, but rather more the sense that I could miss a season of my life. When our snowdrop began to bloom in January, I felt deprived of the joy of anticipation as well as a sense of being hurried through the days. As if, like Rip van Winkle, I might awaken from a short nap to find myself an old man.

Somehow though, the seasons seem to intersperse themselves amidst each other. This year we seemed to have March in January, January in February and touches of February in March. Last year we had April flowers followed by May showers (deluges, in fact). Runners of the Boston Marathon have experienced ninety-degree summer days some years, cold rain or sleet on others. We have all known those late November Indian Summer days which come from year to year. Ten years ago at Easter we enjoyed a seventy-degree Sunday followed by over two feet of snow on Monday and Tuesday. My brother Nigel and his wife Karen, who were visiting from England hoping to see a little remaining snow received more than they had wished for. We celebrated with a belated Christmas dinner on April 1st as the snow coated our windows.

This year Diane and I went once again to the New England Spring Flower Show. We first discovered it in the 1980's and have attended each year since. After digging out from the heavy wet snow of the previous day, we drove to Boston through the wintry landscape. Inside the Expo center, the rich colors and fragrant aromas brought us forward to all that is to come. Nowhere is the confusion of the seasons more apparent than in some of the abundant display gardens there. The various exhibits seemed to represent spring mornings, early summer afternoons, late summer evenings. In some gardens all the seasons came together into one. Hyacinths and hollyhocks bloomed side by side. Daffodils and daylilies were flowering companions alongside crocuses and coreopsis, rhododendrons and rosebushes.

We drove back to Concord through Boston and Cambridge looking at the changes that the city has undergone these last decades: new upscale condominiums tucked between aging apartment buildings, upmarket stores replacing their tired predecessors, Harvard Square populated by students who were yet unborn when I saw it for the first time in 1975.

I still remember clearly being the pony-tailed young man walking for the first time down Massachusetts Avenue, past the Sears and Roebuck at Porter Square, the Cambridge Country Store, Erewhon. The intense heat of an early August afternoon was new to me then. I was at the beginning of my years here. Life stretched out before me almost longer than I could fully imagine. In 1975 I purchased vinyl records at the Harvard Coop, browsed for books in the Paperback Booksmith, watched movies at the Orson Welles cinema.

On a Saturday in June in 1978, my parents first came to this country and together we rode the elevator to the top of the Prudential Tower and looked out over the city and harbor. In the 1980's Diane and I used to ride the train into Boston, change at North Station and travel on to Rockport for a summer weekend. Twenty years ago I ran from Concord's North Bridge to Boston in the inaugural Boston Peace Marathon crossing the Charles River via the Longfellow Bridge on a crisp November afternoon.

On a spring day in 2007, all this past and all this present seemed to coalesce before me like the many seasons simultaneously displayed at the flower show. All that has passed, all that is or is yet to be seeming as one. All the seasons of my life were yet one life, dissolving time.

Now as March turns to April and temperatures slowly begin to warm, as the grass begins to green, as we move from winter to spring, from dormancy to awakening, as one day slips inexorably into another, season following upon season, the lion and the lamb pace watchfully around each other and briefly lie down together.

# AGING PICTURES
## May 2007

Shortly after Mother's Day a couple of years ago, upon returning from a visit to my native England, I compiled an album of old family photographs. Many of them had been tucked into envelopes and stored in a closet for years. Others my brother Nigel had copied onto CDs which he gave to me, and from which I had several prints made. One of the earliest pictures was taken about a hundred years ago, and shows my grandmother as a child standing next to her mother and holding a photograph of her father who was away in the Royal Navy. My grandmother's face in the picture is so remarkably and unmistakably her own that it is almost impossible for me to see a five-year-old child in the frame rather than a miniature version of the grandmother I knew and loved for the first 43 years of my life.

As I turn from page to page in the album, I find pictures of my grandfather returning from service after the First World War, of my mother at age 12, rowing on the Thames in the 1930s. There is a picture of my father, which Nigel found on a trip to Ireland three years ago, when he stopped to visit the boarding school that Dad attended just outside Dublin. On the wall amidst framed photos of successful school rugby teams, he found the 1932-33 championship-winning team with my 16-year-old father sitting cross-legged on the ground in the right foreground. With digital camera in hand he was able to make a copy which he e-mailed to me.

Pictures from my parents' wedding in Oxford in 1949 show them embarking on the new life that was to produce the family in which I grew up. But once again as I look at the photograph I can hardly see them as two people who would be young enough to be my children. I see my parents.

Fading black and white photographs, half-forgotten images from a lost world, yet come alive as memories which I always carry forward. There is a way in which I have always felt a certain timelessness of self, not exactly agelessness as my body from time to time reminds me. Thus, looking at old photographs, the familiar subjects seem in some essential way to be aging right along with me, so that we all keep our place in the natural order of things.

I see the early pictures of myself in situations which I can still recall. Sitting in the open trunk of a family car with both brothers, Sean and Nigel, beside me posing for a commercial photographer advertising the roominess of the new Morris Oxford in 1958. I see the schoolchildren in the playground of my primary schools, one of the first pictures that I took with my new Brownie 127 in 1961. As I look at the boys most of whom I have never seen since we left in 1963, it's as if they have grown older alongside me. I see them eye to eye, as if they too are six feet tall not the little boys that we all were then. In a picture of Sean astride a bicycle on the back lawn of our Oxford house, I see not a twelve-year old boy, but an older brother. Conversely, my mother today still thinks of her fifty-something sons as her boys.

It is baffling to me that all these memories seem so clear to me on the one hand, and yet so obviously distorted, as is my vision of the photographs. I remember well standing on my father's hands as he lifted me toward the sky, I remember cold early winter nights celebrating Guy Fawkes on November 5th with fireworks, Dad making us stand back while he lit Catherine Wheels pinned into the plum tree, set off Roman Candles, fired rockets from milk bottles into the starlit sky, as we stood waving sparklers.

I remember the hours of playing with my brothers on pedal cars and pogo sticks and bicycles, being tended by my mother when I had the flu, but yet I do not recall my child's mind, the thoughts and feelings, such as I observe now in my great nephews who are eight and six. I remember those things through the filter of my present mind, as if the 55-year-old me was in that body having those experiences.

In some way the essence of self is what remains of my internal memory. Similarly, in looking at the hundred-year-old picture of my grandmother, I see the essence of herself, visible at age five, and still to be found 90 years later, before she died in 1995 at age 93. My brothers are always eye to eye, parents always to be looked up to. As for myself, I feel by no means forever young, rather forever me.

As past and present and future seem so mysteriously intertwined, 'then' seems like a part of 'now'. Torn between that which seems constant and that which is ever changing, memory is the crazy glue which holds together this paradox of timeless aging.

—

# A FATHER'S DAY MEMORY
## June 2007

My father always had a certain dreamy optimism. It was partly faith and partly just a willingness to engage in the process of living, to make the best of things, to embrace the life he was given. He was a loving man who always saw the good in others, and always expected things to turn out for the best in the end.

When we bought the corner-shop in Bournemouth in 1964, he was tested quite severely. It turned out to be something of a disaster. Stuck on the corner at the top of the hill, R.J.Leahy and Sons nestled between the unbroken rows of Victorian red-brick houses. From there, he tried to make a living selling groceries to the neighbors on the sleepy street, while at the bottom of the hill the main road beckoned with its new mini supermarkets, shopping carts, green stamps.

The landlord had convinced him it would be a little gold-mine, and with the small print-shop on the adjacent corner needing cheese rolls for their twelve employees five days a week, and cigarettes and other ancillary purchases which would surely grow out of that trade, Dad had had high hopes. The previous tenants were getting out after only two years, but when Dad met with them and Mr. Grouse, the landlord, and their solicitor, Mr. Gay, their books looked good. It would be our little gold-mine. R. J. Leahy & Sons. But he didn't realize that Mrs. Barger from the printers would drive such a hard bargain for her meager supplies, bustling into the shop each morning at 8:30 demanding that everything be ready for her, insisting on the lowest price, threatening to take the feeble lifeline of her business to the shop around the corner.

We were only there for a few months when Dad realized that he would have to look for a job, and leave Mum alone in the store to wait behind the counter for the few customers to trickle in, or to be browbeaten each morning by Mrs. Barger's ill temper.

I think that was when Dad started praying to Saint Jude. "The patron saint of hopeless cases," he called him. I was relieved when Saint Jude did help him to find a job, working in the warehouse down at one of the department stores in the Square. While it was not as good as being a partner back in the family coal business, it did mean that, when with Mr. Gay's help, we eventually sold the business after two years, he was able to pay off most of the creditors with the proceeds.

Gradually he got back on his feet somewhat. Mum's charm bracelet made a few trips to the pawnshop and back. We found a cheap flat where Dad got something off of the rent in return for doing the gardening. We just became accustomed to buying everything on hire purchase. With St. Jude's assistance he did find a slightly better job, and Mum started working, too, until she had the miscarriage. And of course after the hysterectomy she had to convalesce for a while.

Dad used to always say: just as soon we get this or that paid off we'll be in the clear. But televisions broke, school uniforms wore out, second-hand lawn mowers stopped working, somehow something always seemed to happen just as his sights were fixing on some point in time perhaps a month or two down the road, when we would be restored to prosperity.

The car did seem like providence though. The color was unusual. It was two-tone. The dealer told Dad it was called Mountain Rose, although Uncle LLoyd, who never really liked Dad anyway, smirked and called it pink. But it was the license plate that convinced Dad that there was some other hand at work; ERU 49OC. It was their initials, their wedding date, their birthplaces, all come together by some mysterious hand of fate: Elfin & Ricky United '49 Oxford & Cork. It was meant to be.

Dad loved that car. It was a Vauxhall Victor, much classier than our old Morris Minor 2000, even though it did have some miles on it. It was in good condition for its age, too, and, since our new flat was at the top of a hill just like the shop had been, it was easy for me to push it down the hill to get it started on cold mornings before Dad took me to school. Dad used to try to work on it himself whenever it broke down,

143

even though he didn't know much about cars. That's why he was changing the points himself one Saturday. It would not have cost very much to have it done at the garage, but since he had just had to buy a brand new pair of glasses the day before, he felt another expense ought to be avoided. One of his co-workers had told him how to do it, and he had borrowed a manual to be perfectly sure.

Dad was always proud of his do-it-yourself achievements. When he nailed the strip of molding in the corner under the kitchen cabinets to hide the wiring he always referred to it as "my bit of carpentry." So changing the points was a source of great satisfaction. Still there were a few Jesus, Mary and Josephs as he wrestled with it under the hood, and when my older brother Sean stopped on his way out for the afternoon to ask him what he was putting in, he answered hotly, "my blood!" Nevertheless, I could see that glow of satisfaction as he finally fixed it into place. Two beads of perspiration ran one on each side of his forehead. Maybe he would take Mum out for a drink with some of the money he had saved. And in another few months we would have the car paid off, then we really would be in the clear.

"Well, the old man can still learn a few new tricks!" he said to me, as he started to straighten up. He came up just a little too quickly. The hood above his head just caught the corner of his brand new glasses, sending them down onto the gravel driveway. We could hear the glass break as soon as they hit.

I thought he would be angry, but he just looked at them with a sort of resignation before he spoke:

"Sure the Lord giveth with one hand, and taketh away with the other."

# SEASONAL CYCLES
## July 2007

It was thirty-four years ago that I first discovered the delight of early mornings. I was a student in Freiburg in Germany's Black Forest and had just turned twenty-one. Up until that time in my life, I had, like many young people, never even considered the possibility of getting out of bed any earlier than necessary.

I remember my mother always trying to convince my brothers and me that "an hour at night is worth two in the morning," as she vainly attempted to persuade us either not to stay up at night or to rise earlier in the morning. The only time I ever saw the dawn was when, as a small boy on Christmas morning, anticipation always drove us to our parents' bedroom door to ask, "Has he come yet?"

Somehow at twenty-one, living in the picturesque small town of Freiburg, I found myself waking early and rising to walk around the town. I would cross the Dreisam river and walk down the cobbled side streets to the Münsterplatz before the day's traffic started to fill the streets.

The smell of the bakeries, the sounds of the birds in the lemon-fragrant linden tree, the cool of the morning air on my skin awoke me to a new experience of summer mornings. At that time in my life summers still seemed unendingly long. School vacations stretched out deliciously. Life promised to last forever. Even twenty years ago, when I was still in my thirties, Diane and I would ride our bicycles throughout the long and lazy months of summer, and time seemed to advance only slowly.

Now at fifty-five, I find everything has sped up. Watching our garden, I see how fleeting the season of each perennial is. It seems the daffodils have only just left when peonies blast through their exuberant days in June. We are already in the middle of July and the daylilies are at their peak.

Each day we pick off the spent blossoms of yesterday in increasing numbers, but already some have passed their zenith. The golden 'Stella de Oro' has already made its show. The yellow-throated and pink 'Canape' has given way to 'Painted Pink' and 'Gentle Rose' and the frilly 'Dance Ballerina Dance'. At the foot of the driveway our maroon and gold 'Monsignor' and peachy 'Second Thoughts' are in full bloom, while 'Ladykin' is on the ascendant. 'Rosy Returns' bloom beside the garage with the promise of a repeat bloom.

Black-eyed Susans visible from the kitchen window will be like sunshine embodied in flowers for another month. At the back of the house our blue Hydrangea 'Endless Summer' tries to convince us of what we now know is not true. Buds on the heptacodium will be white blossoms in August, red calices in September and October. Every flower has its season. Fleeting and perennial.

Thirty-four years after my Black Forest dawn walks, I have been discovering early mornings on a bicycle in Concord. Riding to work as often as possible to reduce automobile use and to get the exercise, I have enjoyed embracing these summer moments. Once a week on Thursdays, I leave at five o'clock in the morning in order to meet the early delivery at the Natural Gourmet. En route I pass roadside daylilies where yesterday's dried blossoms are giving way to the new flowers just preparing to open for their day in the sun.

Once again I have begun to notice the morning birdsong in its incredible variety. Wheeling along Sudbury Road, I catch the whoops and warbles, trills and twitters, caws and cackles and chirps and chirrups of this invisible world. One morning as I was listening for all the sounds, ignorant of which bird might produce which song, I was lost in a reverie when I almost ran over a wild turkey standing in the middle of the Main Street near the railroad bridge at Coolidge Road. He turned his head as I whisked by, and then he calmly returned to the woodlands from which he had come.

One week later a deer and I surprised each other in almost the same spot. I startled in the saddle of my bike, the deer jumped and stared for the briefest of moments then clattered back up the driveway of the house where it had been standing.

As I coasted into West Concord a few minutes later, I caught sight of a surprise of another kind. In a crack in the tarmac sidewalk right at the railroad crossing, a 'Stella de Oro' daylily had found its opportunity, providing a floral greeting to passers-by at the Junction. Many days since I have watched for its succession of flowers as I cross the railroad track.

It is the middle of summer but already I feel things passing. Independence Day has come and gone. The purple loosestrife, which I first saw on a dawning August morning thirty-two years ago when I arrived in Concord, will soon be ablaze along the riverbank. The days are getting shorter even as they get warmer. Last Saturday on Bastille Day (July 14th) I bought a carton of milk and was dismayed to see that its expiration was Labor Day. My bicycle has twelve speeds which I can somewhat control, but as I cycle through life in a gear which I cannot set, I try to embrace the moments of summer, savor the surprises and stay alert for those wild turkeys.

# LIVING IN CONCORD
## January 2007

Occasionally, if I am awake in the night, I entertain myself with words and numbers. Sometimes, in the stillness and darkness of the predawn hours, I compose poems. Sometimes I do math problems. Last night I was thinking about how long I have lived in Concord, and, as I lay there, I decided to calculate the number of days since I first arrived here in August of 1975. I multiplied the years, factored in eight leap days and added in the remaining days of the first year and the first days of the present year. To my surprise and, I must admit, delight, since I love the symmetries and patterns of round numbers, I discovered that I have been here for exactly 11,500 days. As I write this, I am celebrating, what I might call my eleven-thousand-five-hundredth diurniversary.

In those many days I have undergone a complete change of cells four times and am halfway through the fifth, and yet the face in the old photographs still bears an uncanny resemblance to today. When I go back to England to visit my family, they still know me, as I know them.

This Valentine's Day Diane and I will have been married for between eight and nine thousand days. Looking through our photograph albums, we can see the changes that have been

151

brought by the passage of time. We can also see the constancy, and I think what a remarkable gift it is to be loved for so many thousands of days. Love re-created and nurtured by choice each day.

Transplanted from Ohio and from England, Diane and I have made a life in Concord, and life in Concord has made us. Like the day-lilies in our garden, we have found soil rich enough to grow in, and as we change from day to day, yet some essence remains.

We have lived in our house now for more than 8,000 days. We planted a pear tree the week we moved in. It's about thirty feet tall today. We have become perennial gardeners together. We have learned that some perennials are more perennial than others. Peonies have sulked when moved, columbines have packed their bags and moved themselves. Daffodils have multiplied in some spots, struggled in others. Evening primrose enjoyed ten good years, then left. Black-eyed susans have thrived under the droughty soil beneath the maple trees. Day-lilies have loved the sun and turned into exuberant producers of summer bloom.

So, too, have I found a place to grow. Working with natural foods for thirty years in the same community, writing for *The Concord Journal* for close to ten years, I have forged an identity. My once tender roots have gradually sunk themselves into the New England soil. No native plant, yet I have naturalized in Concord, while still bearing all the traits of my heredity.

When I first moved to the United States, a phone call home could cost a few hours pay. Air travel was a serious consideration. There was no internet. Today, I telephone my mother every Sunday morning, my brothers and I connect by telephone and e-mail. I cross the Atlantic more easily.

When I am here I hold fast to my memories. I am the boy who ran between the rose trellises of our back garden in Oxford, who listened to my father singing ballads of old Ireland, who rode for tuppence ha'penny on the bus into town with my mother, bicycled with my brother Sean to Sandford to see our grandparents, played for countless summer afternoons with my brother Nigel in our flat in Bournemouth. I remember dressing in our blue school uniforms and carrying our satchels to school, Sunday afternoon car rides, summer holidays at the seaside. I remember arguing about which of us would walk up the hill to bring home fish and chips for lunch on Saturdays, and then all going together because we couldn't resolve the question. I remember knowing that I was loved, and learning to love.

I have missed my family for most of these 11,500 days. I have missed seeing my nephew Ryan and niece Fiona growing into young adults. But even as I have missed them all, I have embraced them in some way all the more. I don't know that absence makes the heart grow fonder, but in my case it certainly has made my mind more conscious of my heart's fondness. When my mother made her visit to us in June, we tried to savor every moment. When she left, I embraced the ache in my heart, knowing that to every thing there is a season.

As I have become who I am: a husband, an organic gardener, a lover of nature and the natural, a writer, I always remain a rememberer. The loss of being far from people I love finds consolation in memory. I live in Concord with my memories.

As Diane and I make our life together, nurturing our garden as it blossoms in spring and summer, fades and dies in fall and winter, returns again in spring, we grow together intertwined with love, remembering where we have come from, accepting both the joys and sorrows that life brings, living in Concord.